Moneywise

Guide to Tax

OTHER TITLES IN THIS SERIES INCLUDE

Moneywise Guide to Your Pension

Moneywise Guide to Planning Your Finances

Moneywise Guide to Investing in the Stockmarket

Moneywise

Guide to Tax

JO HANKS

RD Publications Ltd · London

in association with

Prentice Hall Europe

London   New York   Toronto   Sydney   Tokyo   Singapore   Madrid
Mexico City   Munich   Paris

Copyright © The Reader's Digest Association Limited, 1998

® Moneywise, Reader's Digest and the Pegasus logo are registered trademarks of
The Reader's Digest Association, Inc. of Pleasantsville, New York, USA.

All rights reserved. No part of this publication may be reproduced, stored in a retrieval system,
or transmitted, in any form or by any means, electronic or mechanical, by photocopying,
recording or otherwise, without prior permission from the copyright holder.

First published 1998 by
Prentice Hall Europe
Campus 400, Maylands Avenue
Hemel Hempstead
Hertfordshire HP2 7EZ
A division of
Simon & Schuster International Group

Every possible care has been taken to ensure the accuracy of the information
in this book, but no responsibility can be accepted for the consequences
of actions based on the advice contained therein. Readers are encouraged
to take relevant professional advice based on personal circumstances.

Editorial and design:
Brown Packaging Books Ltd
Bradley's Close
74–77 White Lion Street
London N1 9PF

Design:
Kingfisher Design, London N2 9NR

Printed and bound in Great Britain by:
T.J. International Ltd, Padstow

Library of Congress Cataloging-in-Publication Data

Available from the publisher

British Library Cataloguing in Publication Data

A Catalogue record for this book is available from the British Library

ISBN: 0-13-911058-5

1 2 3 4 5   03 01 00 99 98

Contents

Ask the Professionals	IX
Preface	X
1 Why it pays to know about tax	12
2 Background and basics	20
THE TAX TIMETABLE	22
WHAT YOU PAY TAX ON	23
WHAT YOU DON'T PAY TAX ON	24
GOOD HOUSEKEEPING	25
3 You and the Inland Revenue	26
THE PAPERWORK	28
PENALTIES	30
4 Your home and your family	36
YOUR HOME	44

v

5 Work — 50
- IF YOU'RE EMPLOYED — 51
- IF YOU'RE SELF-EMPLOYED — 60
- NATIONAL INSURANCE — 65

6 Savings and investments — 68
- TAX ON UK INVESTMENTS — 71
- DEPOSIT-BASED SAVINGS — 72
- FIXED-INTEREST INVESTMENTS — 78
- INSURANCE-BASED INVESTMENTS — 80
- STOCKMARKET INVESTMENTS — 85
- OTHER INVESTMENTS — 89
- HOW TO SAVE MORE ON TAX INVESTMENTS — 90
- OFFSHORE INVESTMENTS — 92

7 Pensions — 94
- TAX RELIEF ON CONTRIBUTIONS — 96
- TAX ON PENSION INVESTMENTS — 98
- TAX ON PENSION INCOME — 99
- STATE PENSIONS — 101
- EMPLOYERS PENSIONS — 102
- PERSONAL PENSIONS — 110

8 Capital gains tax — 122

9 Inheritance tax — 132

- **Cutting your IHT bill** — 135
- **Using life insurance to pay the bill** — 140
- **Putting plans into practice** — 140
- **Working out the value of your estate** — 141

10 Filling in your tax return — 142

- **Employment supplementary pages** — 147
- **Employment supplementary pages continued** — 149
- **Share schemes supplementary pages** — 151
- **Share schemes supplementary pages continued** — 153
- **Self-employment supplementary pages** — 155
- **Self-employment supplementary pages continued** — 157
- **Self-employment suplementary pages continued** — 159
- **Self-employment supplementary pages continued** — 161
- **Land and property supplementary pages** — 163
- **Land and propert supplementary pages continued** — 165
- **Capital gains supplementary pages** — 167
- **Tax return page 3: Income** — 169
- **Tax return page 4: Income continued** — 171
- **Tax return page 5: Reliefs** — 173
- **Tax return page 6: Allowances** — 175
- **Tax return page 7: Other information** — 177
- **Tax return page 8: Other information continued** — 179

VII

11 Working out your income tax bill — 180
The calculations — 181
Help! — 185

12 Complaints and tax return enquiries — 186

13 Inland revenue leaflets — 194
Personal taxpayer series — 195
Business series — 202
Capital Taxes Office series — 204
International series — 204
Clubs and charities series — 204
Codes of Practice — 205
The Adjudicator's Office — 205

An A–Z guide to financial words and phrases — 206

Directory — 209

Index — 212

About the Moneywise Ask the Professionals panel...

THROUGHOUT THIS BOOK you will find comments and explanations from members of the *Moneywise* Ask the Professionals panel. The members are authorised professional advisers specialising in different areas of financial planning who answer *Moneywise* readers' letters every month. The panel aims to answer any financial queries. The service is free and using it puts you under no obligation whatsoever.

For advice write to:
'Ask the Professionals'
Moneywise
11 Westferry Circus
Canary Wharf
London E14 4HE

JANET ADAM is a tax partner at chartered accountants BDO Stoy Hayward, based in Manchester

WALTER AVRILI is operations director at independent mortgage advisers John Charcol in London

BRIAN DENNEHY is an independent financial adviser and managing director of Dennehy, Weller & Co in Kent

KEAN SEAGER is an independent financial adviser and managing director of Whitechurch Securities in Bristol

KEITH SANHAM is an independent financial adviser at Fairmount Trust Plc, based in Leatherhead, Surrey

REBEKAH KEAREY is an independent financial adviser and a partner at Roundhill Financial Management in Brighton

Preface

You've just got past the biggest difficulty most people face with their finances. You've got past page 1 – and you're still reading. With most financial literature, that's unusual. Fear, fatigue or frustration would normally have set in by now – caused by figures, jargon, cf paragraph C sub-section three ... and more figures.  That's why most financial books go unread, why most bank statements go unopened ... why most self-assessment tax-returns go back late.

But money doesn't have to be that difficult. If you flick through some of these pages, you'll be looking at flowcharts that show your financial choices in simple terms. And with a *Moneywise* publication, that's not unusual. *Moneywise* has always set out to make money make sense – key facts and figures, plain English, clear headings and action points. That's why *Moneywise* is Britain's best-read personal finance magazine ... and probably why you opened this book.

And now that you've started, you'll find it gets easier. As you read more pages of these *Moneywise* guides, you'll get to know more about financial planning, pensions, tax and stockmarket investments. You'll find that this knowedge really does give you power. You'll know what to ask, what to look for and what to expect when you deal with financial companies. You may start by following our action points but go on to work out your own!

All the action points and flowcharts in our guides have been put together with this aim in mind. We asked leading independent financial advisers (IFAs) and *Moneywise*'s award-winning financial journalists to provide you with up-to-date practical advice – not textbook tax book theory.

It's all just over the page. So get past this preface and get to the advice you need. But if you're still standing in the bookshop reading this, go via the cash desk – you'll find this is an investment that will really pay off.

Matthew Vincent

Matthew Vincent
Editor
Moneywise

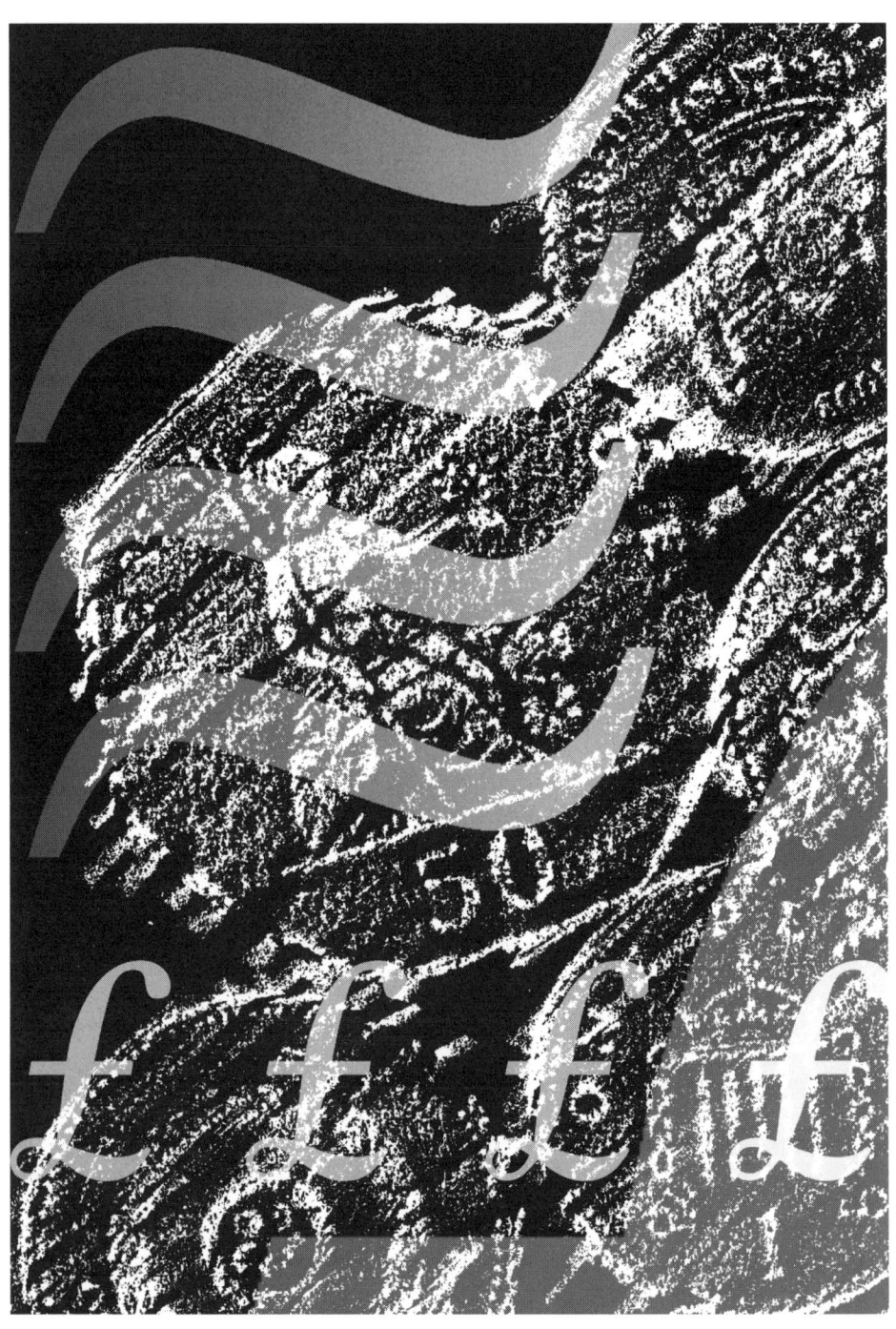

1 Why it pays to know about tax

No one buys a book about tax for fun, and no matter how hard the Inland Revenue tries to appeal to us with Hector the cartoon tax inspector, it's not a subject you'll find very many people laughing about.

Tax is a fact of life and regardless of your views on whether some of us should pay more or less, none of us want to pay more than is required under the rules. And unfortunately the rules can be very complicated.

On top of this, you may have received a new-style tax return this year; even if you didn't you cannot have failed to hear about the new system called self assessment.

One aim of this book is to answer some of the more general questions regarding tax, such as:

○ Do I need to worry about self assessment?
○ Could I be paying too much tax?
○ What taxes do I have to pay and when?
○ How can I make sure my savings and investments are tax-efficient?
○ Will I get a tax return and when do I have to fill it in?

Another aim is to answer any more specific technical questions you may may have.

The flowcharts on the following pages give the basic answers to some of these questions, and direct you to the places in the chapters which cover the subjects in detail.

Self assessment

If you were to believe many accountants and tax consultants there isn't a person in the land who doesn't need to worry about self assessment. The Inland Revenue, probably rightly, made a great song and dance about the new system, which succeeded in striking fear into the hearts of many a taxpayer – and in delighting the professionals who knew they could convince people their services were now more useful than ever.

But many people can certainly manage without them. This book explains the new rules and requirements under self assessment. These relate to when you have to pay tax, the kinds of records you need to keep and penalties for missing deadlines or failing to keep records. And, if you want to, you can work out your tax bill yourself. You don't have to and the Inland Revenue has now decided it would make its work easier if you didn't, but this doesn't mean that there will not come a time when working it out yourself becomes compulsory. Now is a good time to get to grips with the rules, so if that time does come, you'll have a head start on everyone else.

Too much tax?

You could well be paying too much tax. The Inland Revenue is sitting on literally billions of pounds to which it's not entitled, and some of that money could be yours. The money includes unclaimed allowances and unused tax relief – the flowchart on page 16 could point you in the direction of any you are missing out on.

Types of taxes

This book deals with three main taxes – income tax, capital gains tax (CGT) and inheritance tax (IHT) – and touches on value added tax (VAT) for the self-employed. All of us need to be aware of income tax rules. The flowchart on page 17 will show you whether you need to know about CGT or IHT.

This book also covers the rules in place for the 1997/98 tax year and helps you fill in your 1996/97 tax return if you haven't already done it (see Chapter 10). It doesn't only cover the specific rules and regulations that apply to your financial arrangements – in Chapters 3 and 12 you will find useful advice and information on how to communicate with the Inland Revenue, how it should treat you, and what to do if things go wrong.

Tax-efficient savings and investments

There are ways of sheltering your hard-earned savings and investments from tax. And even non-taxpayers can benefit from knowing the tax rules on investments. The flowchart on page 18 directs you to the types of tax-efficient investments that might suit you.

Tax returns

The new system of self assessment doesn't mean that people who haven't received a tax return in the past will get one now. If you do get one and you haven't had one before it will either be because you now fit in to one of the categories of people who receive tax returns, or because you have been selected at random. The Inland Revenue sends out about nine million tax returns each year, and the flowchart on page 19 indicates whether you are likely to receive one. There may be instances where you need to ask for a tax return, and these are explained in Chapter 3.

Remember, you do not have to be earning or sitting on a fortune to benefit from tax-planning arrangements. Even the most simple financial transactions, such as opening a savings account, have tax implications, so it pays to know what they are. Let us know if reading this book pays off.

You're paying too much tax

- If the Inland Revenue gets your PAYE code wrong.
- If your savings and investments aren't tax efficient.
- If you're self-employed and not claiming for all the right allowable expenses and capital allowances.
- If you're married and don't divide the savings and investments and allowances tax efficiently.
- If you don't shelter your wealth from inheritance tax.
- If you don't take advantage of the annual capital gains tax exemption

Could you be paying too much tax?

Are you married?

- **Yes** → You are entitled to the married couple's allowance. You can rearrange ownership of savings and investments to keep your joint tax bill down (see Chapter 4).
- **No** → **Are you separated or divorced?**
  - **Yes** → Certain maintenance payments are tax free. You can get tax relief on some maintenance payments you make (see Chapter 4).
  - **No** →

Are you employed or self-employed?

- **Employed** → You can get tax relief on contributions to your employer's pension scheme or a personal pension (see Chapter 7). If you have a company car, the tax you pay on it may make buying your own car a better option (See Chapter 5).
- **Self-employed** → You can claim allowable expenses and capital allowances to cut your taxable profits (see chapter 5). You can get tax relief on contributions to a personal pension (see chapter 7).
- **Neither**

Are you over 65?

- **Yes** → You could be entitled to higher allowances (see Chapter 4).
- **No** →

Do you have any savings and investments?

- **Yes** → You can get tax breaks on different types of investment. See the flowchart on page 18 and Chapter 6.
- **No** → When you start saving, remember to see if you would benefit from the tax-free types of investment. See the flowchart on page 18 and Chapter 6.

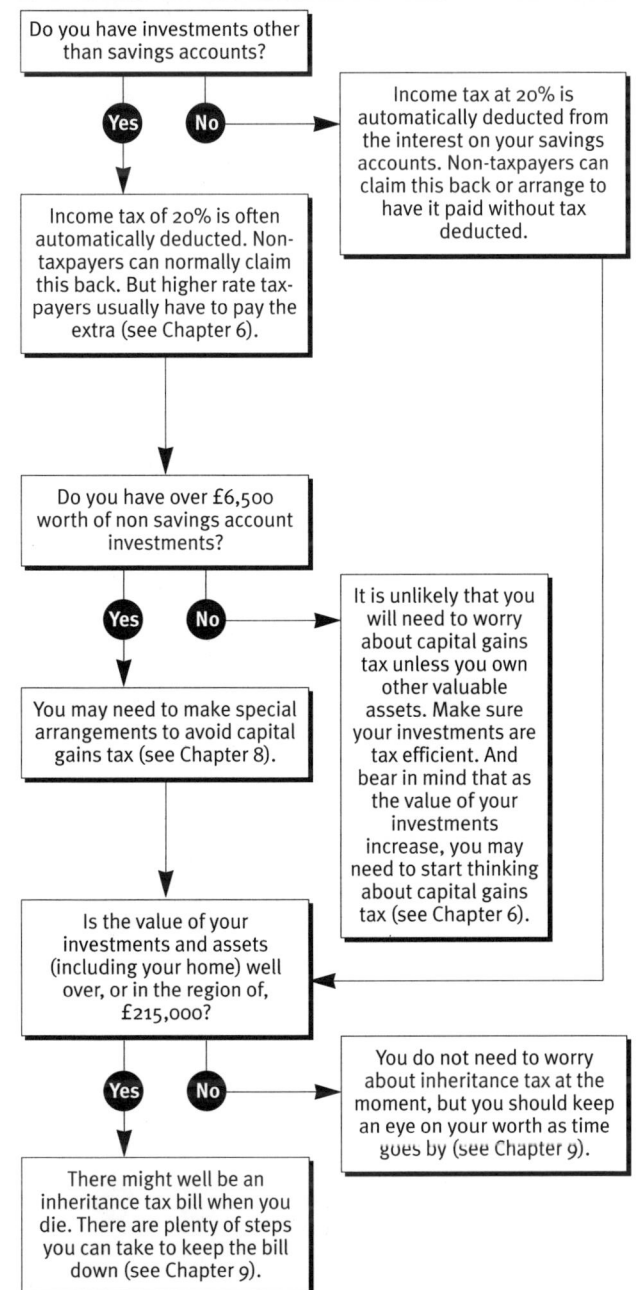

Tax-efficient savings and investments

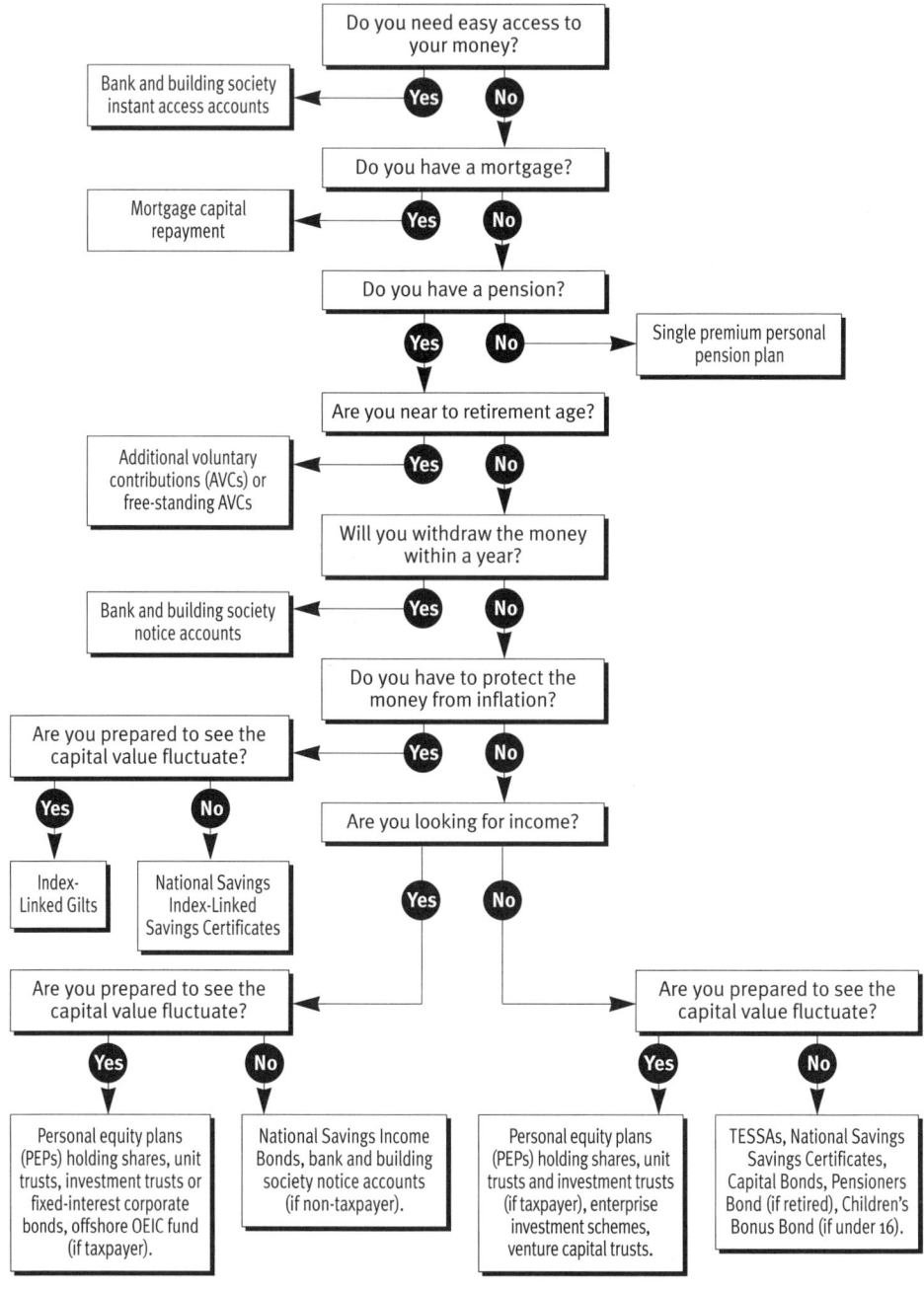

Do you need easy access to your money?
- **Yes** → Bank and building society instant access accounts
- **No** ↓

Do you have a mortgage?
- **Yes** → Mortgage capital repayment
- **No** ↓

Do you have a pension?
- **Yes** ↓
- **No** → Single premium personal pension plan

Are you near to retirement age?
- **Yes** → Additional voluntary contributions (AVCs) or free-standing AVCs
- **No** ↓

Will you withdraw the money within a year?
- **Yes** → Bank and building society notice accounts
- **No** ↓

Do you have to protect the money from inflation?
- **Yes** → Are you prepared to see the capital value fluctuate?
  - **Yes** → Index-Linked Gilts
  - **No** → National Savings Index-Linked Savings Certificates
- **No** ↓

Are you looking for income?
- **Yes** → **Are you prepared to see the capital value fluctuate?**
  - **Yes** → Personal equity plans (PEPs) holding shares, unit trusts, investment trusts or fixed-interest corporate bonds, offshore OEIC fund (if taxpayer).
  - **No** → National Savings Income Bonds, bank and building society notice accounts (if non-taxpayer).
- **No** → **Are you prepared to see the capital value fluctuate?**
  - **Yes** → Personal equity plans (PEPs) holding shares, unit trusts and investment trusts (if taxpayer), enterprise investment schemes, venture capital trusts.
  - **No** → TESSAs, National Savings Savings Certificates, Capital Bonds, Pensioners Bond (if retired), Children's Bonus Bond (if under 16).

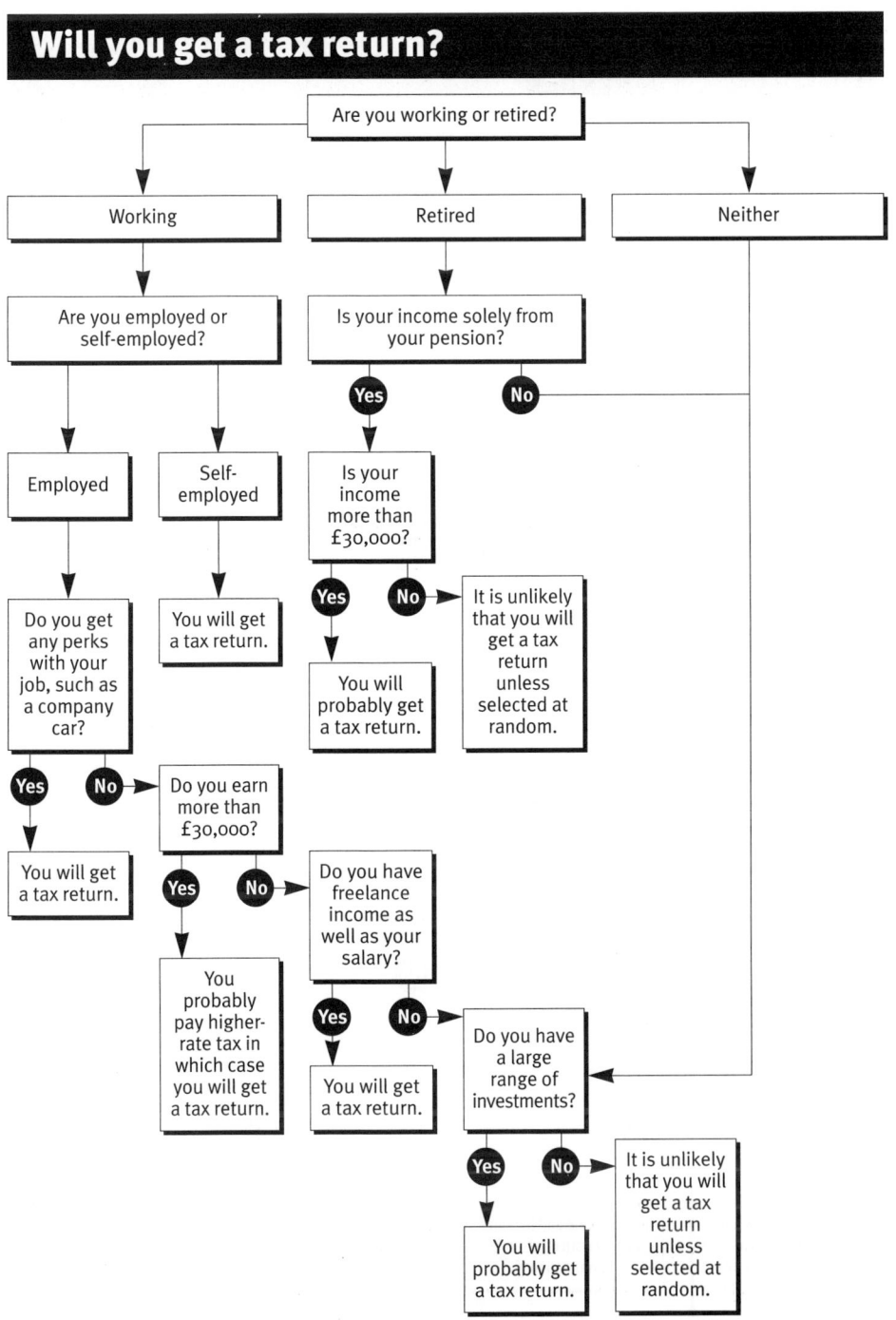

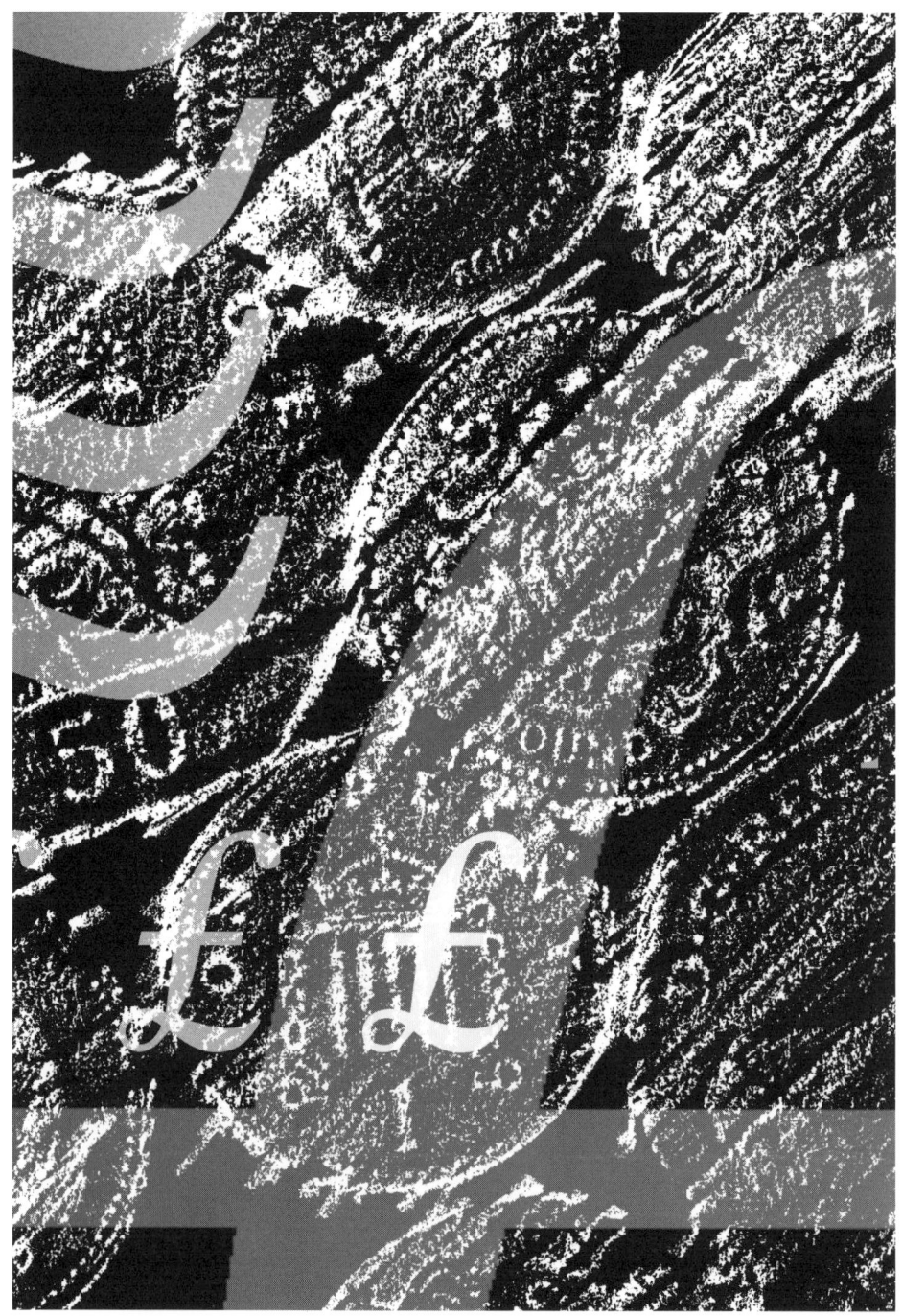

2 Background and basics

If you're unfamiliar with the basic ideas behind the tax system, this chapter provides the help you need by covering some of the basics of the system which will help you understand the more detailed tax rules and use them to your advantage.

Tax goes back a long way. The origins of the Inland Revenue as a department go back to 1694 when the Board of Commissioners of Stamps was set up to administer the newly introduced stamp duty. Income tax was introduced to help pay for the Napoleonic Wars, and resurfaced in the mid-19th century. The Board of Inland Revenue was set up in 1849.

Income tax now makes up nearly a quarter of the government's revenue. The pie chart below shows the expected sources of government income in 1997/98.

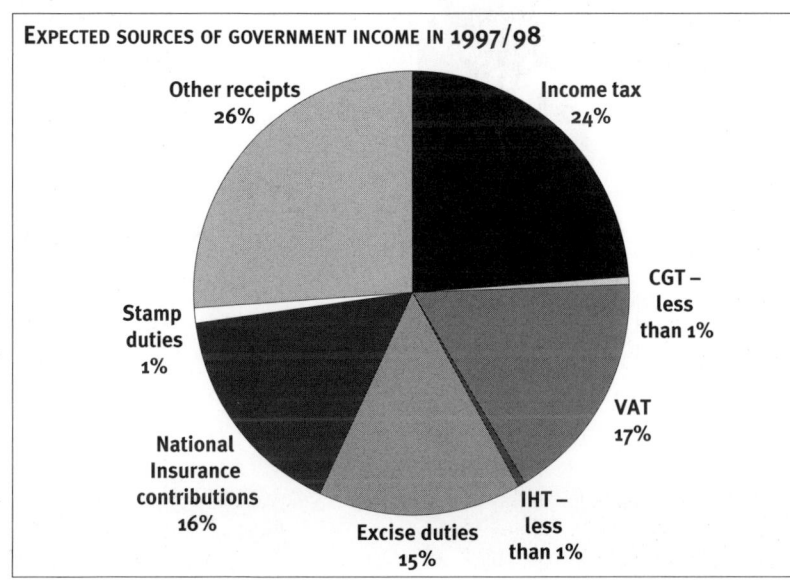

EXPECTED SOURCES OF GOVERNMENT INCOME IN 1997/98
- Other receipts 26%
- Income tax 24%
- CGT – less than 1%
- VAT 17%
- IHT – less than 1%
- Excise duties 15%
- National Insurance contributions 16%
- Stamp duties 1%

21

The tax timetable

THE INLAND REVENUE works to a slightly different calendar than the rest of us. For historical reasons the tax year runs from 6 April in one calendar year to 5 April in the next.

This book is about the rules which apply for the tax year from 6 April 1997 to 5 April 1998, which we will call the 1997/98 tax year. We will also cover some of the changes introduced in Chancellor Gordon Brown's July Budget, which take effect from the beginning of the 1998/99 tax year (from 6 April 1998).

Changes to tax rules and rates are announced in the Budget every year. In recent years Budgets have taken place at the end of November. At the time this book was published, Gordon Brown had decided to revert to the previous system of delivering a Budget in March, so look out for a spring 1998 Budget.

Where you have a choice of tax treatment, you need to be aware of the time limits for letting the Inland Revenue know. For example, if you're married and wish to share the married couple's allowance between you and your partner, you need to complete form 18 and send it to your tax office by the beginning of the tax year for which you want it to apply. This will remain in force until you tell your tax office otherwise (see Chapter 4). And there are time limits for using up losses if you're self-employed (see Chapter 5).

If you've forgotten to claim allowances or tax relief in the past, they are, at present, not lost forever until six tax years later. So, provided you contact the Inland Revenue about them before 6 April 1998, you can claim for missed allowances as far back as the 1991/92 tax year, but you can claim only the amounts that applied at the time. This rule is changing in 2002. For timetables of when to complete your tax return and when you have to pay tax, see pages 32–5.

What you pay tax on

THE TAXES COVERED in this book are income tax, capital gains tax (CGT) and inheritance tax (IHT) – what you pay those taxes on is fairly self-explanatory:

- You pay income tax on income – whether it is from a job, self-employment, or from investments.
- You pay capital gains tax on any increase in the value of assets and investments over the time you own them.
- Inheritance tax is levied on the value of assets and investments belonging to you on your death and on certain gifts made during your lifetime.

TAX RATES

As explained opposite, tax rates are set in the annual Budget for the following tax year. They don't always change. For the 1997/98 tax year there are three rates of income tax, which you have to pay on different levels of income:

Income up to £4,100	*Lower rate*	20%
Income between £4,100 and £26,100	*Basic rate*	23%
Income over £26,100	*Higher rate*	40%

For capital gains tax, the relevant amount is added to your taxable income to establish the rate at which you pay tax (see Chapter 8). The rate of IHT depends on when it is levied and, possibly, on the part of your taxable estate it applies to – the basic rule is 40% for the 1997/98 tax year (see Chapter 9).

You may hear the term 'marginal rate' of tax – this simply means the top rate of tax that you have to pay. For example, if your taxable income is £10,000, it falls within the basic-rate band, and you pay tax at 20% on the first £4,100 and at 23% on the balance (£5,900). Your top – or marginal – rate of tax is 23%. Other terms you are likely to come across are 'gross' and 'net'; gross simply means before tax while net means after tax.

> **EXAMPLE**
> If you have a savings account, tax is charged on the interest at 20%, and is deducted automatically before the interest is credited to your account. Say your account pays 5% gross, on £10,000 you'd be entitled to £500 gross interest. Once tax is deducted, the net amount you'd receive would be £400 (20% of £500 is £100, £500 less £100 is £400).

What you don't pay tax on

THERE ARE MANY REASONS why some of your income, capital gains, or estate can be excluded from or deducted in the calculation of the relevant tax bill. Most of these are dealt with in greater detail in the rest of the book, and include the following:

- You are allowed a certain amount of tax-free income.
- You get a slight discount on mortgage interest.
- There is no CGT to pay when you sell your main home.
- You can make £6,500-worth of capital gains tax-free.
- Parents and grandparents of people getting married can give certain tax-free gifts.
- There is no tax to pay on anything that you give your husband or wife.
- There is no IHT to pay on the first £215,000 of your estate.
- Investments in personal equity plans (PEPs) are free of income tax and CGT.
- Interest on your savings in a tax-exempt special savings account (TESSA) is tax free.
- There is no CGT to pay when you sell gilts.
- You get tax relief on contributions to a pension.
- Under the rent-a-room scheme you can receive up to £4,250 in rent tax free.
- Certain National Savings investments provide a tax-free return.

CHARITY

There are various tax-efficient ways to give to charity, which benefit both you and your chosen charities. You can open a 'charity account' with the Charities Aid Foundation (CAF) and pay into it via the 'give as you earn' (GAYE) scheme, a covenant or 'Gift Aid'.

Deed of covenant: This is a legally binding agreement to give part of your income to a charity each year. It attracts tax relief if you sign up for more than three years. For example, if you want to give a charity £100 you sign a covenant agreeing to pay £77 and the charity can claim back £23 from the Inland Revenue. If you are a higher-rate taxpayer, you can claim the additional tax relief for yourself.

Give as you earn: GAYE schemes allow employees to get income tax relief at their top rate on donations of up to £900 a year. The money is paid to the charity from your gross pay.

Gift Aid: Under this scheme you can get tax relief on gifts to charity of at least £250. You claim the relief through your tax return, so you have to pay a net amount of at least £250.

If you have at least £10,000 to donate to charity, find out about setting up a charitable trust; the CAF can help you with this.

Good housekeeping

It's worth getting into good habits as far as keeping financial records is concerned. If you've been filling in tax returns for years you will probably have learned the benefit of this, and if you are self-employed you'd find it hard to keep on top of things if you didn't. With self assessment it becomes all the more important – there is now a legal requirement to keep records in support of the information you give on your tax return.

Some documents you need to hold on to

- Tax vouchers that come with share dividends, unit trust distributions and gilt interest payments.

- Contract notes/investment statements received when you buy or sell gilts.

- Records of any payment received from a trust.

- Amounts of taxable maintenance received.

- Copy of your P45 when you leave your job.

- P60 from either your employer or pension provider.

- Copy of the P11D your employer sends to the Revenue.

- Annual statement of interest earned on bank and building society accounts

- If you contribute to a personal pension, pension plan contributions certificate from the pension provider.

You'll find out more about why you need to keep these documents in the relevant chapters and in Chapter 10.

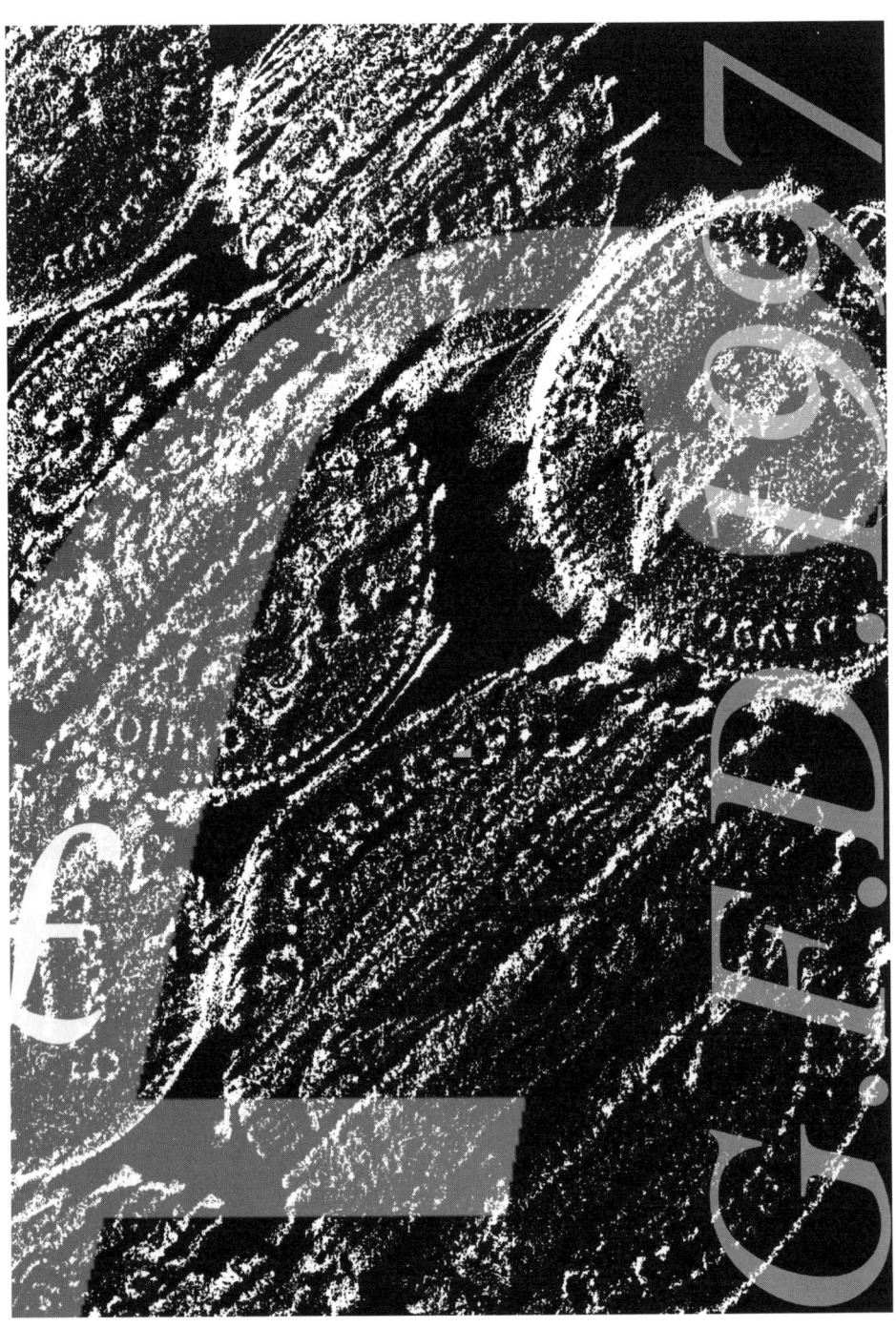

3 You and the Inland Revenue

The Inland Revenue is just over halfway through a ten-year programme of modernisation and improvement. This covers four key areas: simplifying and streamlining work processes, reorganising local offices, making better use of information technology, and improving management of work and people.

Your tax office

The reorganisation of local offices means that all your tax affairs should be handled by one tax office. If this hasn't been possible, the Inland Revenue will provide you with one point of contact, so that any chasing around that has to be done is the responsibility of the Inland Revenue, and not yours. The basic rules for establishing which tax office it is that deals with your affairs are as follows:

○ If you're employed, your employer will be able to tell you the name and address of your tax office – if you move jobs, your tax office may change.
○ If you become unemployed you stay with the tax office relating to your last employer.
○ If you're self-employed or in a partnership, your tax office is usually the one nearest to where you work. If your income is from an employers pension, your tax office will probably be the one in the area where the pension fund office is. If it's only a small pension or your only pension is from the State, it will be the office in the area in which you live.

Tax expert and *Moneywise* Ask the Professionals panellist Janet Adam says:

"The Inland Revenue intends streamlining its organisation, which should result in additional help and advice for taxpayers via telephone helplines and tax enquiry centres with longer opening hours. Larger specialised groups within tax offices will ensure that efforts to collect unpaid tax are concentrated in those areas where traditionally the Inland Revenue feels the Exchequer has lost out."

- If your only income is from a personal pension, your tax office will be the one that covers the pension provider.
- If your only income is from investments, where the office is will depend on where you live.

GETTING INFORMATION

Apart from getting help from your own tax office, there are 312 tax enquiry centres around the country. Any Inland Revenue office should be able to help you or point you in the right direction. You can find addresses in the telephone book under 'Inland Revenue'. If you want detailed information about capital gains tax or inheritance tax the capital taxes offices are happy to help too (see the Directory on page 215–25). There are plenty of free leaflets available, and some of those which are most useful for individual taxpayers are listed on pages 205–15. It is important to remember that you need to keep the Inland Revenue informed of any changes in your circumstances, for example if you get married.

The paperwork

INLAND REVENUE PAPERWORK

The Inland Revenue may send you formal documents. If you're employed or on a pension, tax may be collected through the 'pay as you earn' (PAYE) system, which means tax is deducted from the income you are due before it's paid to you.

The amount deducted is based on a code. For more details on this see Chapter 5. You are informed of your code with a 'notice of coding'.

If you are self-employed, you will of course receive a tax return. Higher-rate taxpayers and employed people with more complex financial arrangements will also receive a tax return each year. As part of the Inland Revenue's modernisation programme and the introduction of self assessment, the tax return changed significantly for the 1996/97 tax year. For more information on the new return and advice about how to complete it, see Chapter 10.

Under the new system you have the choice of whether or not to work out your tax bill yourself – the new tax return includes a section on working out your bill. Chapter 11 gives you an idea of how this is done. But as we explain in Chapter 10, there is no pressure to do the calculations yourself, so unless you're prepared to spend the time or pay an accountant, it's probably best left to the Inland Revenue.

If you don't want to work out your tax bill yourself, you have to send back your tax return by 30 September. You will then receive a 'notice of calculation', which shows how your tax liability has been worked out and tells you how much you have to pay and when. If there is any tax outstanding it will have to be paid by 31 January of the following year.

If you do work out the bill yourself, the deadline for sending back the return along with any tax that you think may be due is 31 January. If you want to work out your bill, but want the tax due collected through PAYE, you must send back the return by 30 September.

The new system requires you to make 'payments on account' on 31 January and 31 July (unless all your tax is being collected through PAYE). So, for example, for the 1998/99 tax year you have to make payments on 31 January and 31 July based on your tax bill for the 1997/98 tax year. Then, based on your return for the 1998/99 tax year, the Revenue (or you) can work out whether there is more tax to pay, or whether you're entitled to a rebate.

If you're sure that you won't need to pay as much tax for the following year as you did in the current year, you can ask to make lower payments on account. You have to write to your tax office to justify the reduction.

> Independent financial adviser and *Moneywise* Ask the Professionals panellist Kean Seager says:
>
> "The Revenue used to be fairly reasonable about filing dates but this is no longer the case. There are no longer 'days of grace' and final dates are final dates."

You'll receive a 'statement of account' about 35 days before 31 January and 31 July to remind you to pay; this will also show any payments made or rebates issued – a bit like a bank or credit card statement. If the outstanding amount is more than £500, you'll receive a statement of account every month until it is paid. If the amount is less than £500, you'll receive a statement of account twice a year.

If you don't send back your tax return, you'll still receive a statement of account, once the penalties start totting up (see page 30).

The calendars on pages 32–3 and 34–5 give a rough idea of what should happen and when, but it is important to understand that much hinges on when you send back your tax return. The calendar does not include possible dates for when you might receive any rebates due. The Inland Revenue will repay any tax you should not have paid with interest – unless it was tax you were legally obliged to pay. So, a rebate due because your two payments on account based on the previous year's bill proved to be too much, would not attract interest.

YOUR PAPERWORK

It's a good idea to keep copies of anything you send to the Inland Revenue, and there are new rules for record-keeping now that self assessment has been introduced. You must keep relevant documents for 22 months after the end of the tax year to which they relate. If you are self-employed or a partner you must keep records for five years after the date you send back your tax return.

The Inland Revenue may decide it wants to make further enquiries into your return; for how this works see Chapter 12. Remember, there may be occasions when you should ask for a tax return so that you can make sure the Inland Revenue knows about all of your income – for example if you start doing freelance work on top of your normal job.

Penalties

THERE ARE NO FINES if you miss the 30 September tax return deadline for those people requiring the Inland Revenue to work out the bill. You have until 31 January before any penalties kick in. But the Inland Revenue cannot guarantee to work out your bill in time for you to pay it in time.

If you miss the 31 January deadline for sending back your tax return, there is an automatic penalty of £100. A further £100 penalty will be imposed if you still haven't sent back your return six months later, by 30 June.

If you don't pay tax on time, you will be charged interest on top. If you haven't paid the tax by 28 February (of the same year), you have to pay a surcharge of 5% of the tax due. If the tax is still outstanding by 31 July, there's another 5% surcharge, as well as the interest that's mounting up.

The Inland Revenue can charge a penalty of up to £3,000 for failure to keep adequate records. In practice it would impose the maximum fine only if someone had wilfully destroyed documents.

You can appeal against penalties. For how to sort out any problems you have with the Inland Revenue, see Chapter 12. The Taxpayer's Charter below lists the standards of 'service' you are entitled to expect.

The Taxpayer's Charter

You are entitled to expect the Inland Revenue:

TO BE FAIR
- By settling your tax affairs impartially.
- By expecting you to pay only what is due under the law.
- By treating everyone with equal fairness.

TO HELP YOU
- To get your tax affairs right.
- To understand your rights and obligations.
- By providing clear leaflets and forms.
- By giving you information and assistance at our enquiry offices.
- By being courteous at all times.

TO PROVIDE AN EFFICIENT SERVICE
- By settling your tax affairs promptly and accurately.
- By keeping your private affairs strictly confidential.

- By using the information you give us only as allowed by the law.
- By keeping to a minimum your costs of complying with the law.
- By keeping our costs down.

TO BE ACCOUNTABLE FOR WHAT WE DO
- By setting standards for ourselves and publishing how well we live up to them.

IF YOU ARE NOT SATISFIED
- We will tell you exactly how to complain.
- You can ask for your tax affairs to be looked at again.
- You can appeal to an independent tribunal.
- Your MP can refer your complaint to the Ombudsman.

IN RETURN, WE NEED YOU
- To be honest.
- To give us accurate information.
- To pay your tax on time.

Tax calendar for the employed

If the Inland Revenue is working out your tax bill

Jan/Feb 1998	Receive notice of coding.
By 31 January 1998	If necessary make first payment on account for 1997/98 tax year (based on tax bill for 1996/97).
April 1998	Receive 1997/98 tax return.
May 1998	Receive form P60 from employer showing pay and tax for 1997/98.
July 1998	Receive form P11D from employer showing details of expenses and taxable perks.
By 31 July 1998	Receive statement of account reminding you to make second payment on account for 1997/98 tax year (based on tax bill for 1996/97).
30 September 1998	Deadline for 1997/98 tax return. Request any tax due to be collected through PAYE if less than £1,000 if preferred.
Autumn 1998	Receive tax calculation from Inland Revenue showing tax bill or rebate due for 1997/98.
January 1999	Receive statement of account showing any tax due and confirming that it will be collected through PAYE, if under £1,000. Receive notice of coding for 1998/99, which will include adjustment to collect the tax.
31 January 1999	Deadline for payment if the outstanding 1997/98 tax is not being collected through PAYE. Make first payment on account for 1998/99 tax year (based on tax bill for 1997/98).

If you are working out your tax bill

Receive notice of coding.

Deadline for 1996/97 tax return and for payment of any outstanding tax (unless being collected through PAYE). If necessary, make first payment on account for 1997/98 tax year (based on tax bill for 1996/97).

Receive 1997/98 tax return.

Receive form P60 from employer showing pay and tax for 1997/98.

Receive form P11D from employer showing details of expenses and taxable perks.

Receive statement of account reminding you to make second payment on account for 1997/98 tax year (based on tax bill for 1996/97), if necessary.

Deadline for 1997/98 tax return if you want the tax due to be collected through PAYE.

Receive statement of account. If you have already sent back return, this will show the tax or rebate due for 1997/98. It will indicate whether the tax will be collected through PAYE if you requested this and sent back the tax return by 30 September 1998. If you haven't sent back your return this acts as a reminder that it is due back by end of the month, along with any outstanding tax.

Send back tax return for 1997/98 along with any outstanding tax.
If necessary, make first payment on account for 1998/99 tax year (based on tax bill for 1997/98).

Tax calendar for the self-employed

If the Inland Revenue is working out your tax bill

By 31 January 1998	Pay any tax outstanding for 1996/97. Make first payment on account for 1997/98 tax year (based on tax bill for 1996/97).
April 1998	Receive tax return for 1997/98 tax year.
By 31 July 1998	Receive statement of account reminding you to make second payment on account for 1997/98 tax year (based on tax bill for 1996/97).
30 September 1998	Deadline for sending back 1997/98 tax return.
Autumn 1998	Receive tax calculation from Inland Revenue, showing total bill for 1997/98, and based on this, the two payments on account for the 1998/99 tax year, which will be due in January and July 1999.
January 1999	Receive statement of account showing any final payment due for 1997/98, or rebate due and the amount of the payment on account due on 31 January 1999.
By 31 January 1999	Make any final payment for 1997/98 tax year, and make first payment on account for 1998/99 tax year.
April 1999	Receive tax return for 1998/99 tax year.

If you are working out your tax bill

Send back tax return for 1996/97 along with any tax outstanding, and make first payment on account for 1997/98 tax year (based on tax bill for 1996/97).

Receive tax return for 1997/98 tax year.

Receive statement of account, reminding you to make second payment on account for 1997/98 tax year (based on tax bill for 1996/97).

Receive statement of account. If you have already sent back your tax return, this will show the tax or rebate due for 1997/98. If you have not sent back your return, this acts as a reminder that it is due back by the end of the month, along with any outstanding tax.

Send back tax return for 1997/98 along with any outstanding tax, and make first payment on account for 1998/99 tax year (based on tax bill for 1997/98).

Receive tax return for 1998/99 tax year.

4 Your home and your family

Your domestic circumstances can have a big influence on your tax bill. Married couples and people over 65 may be entitled to extra tax-free income, for example. And there are special tax rules for home owners.

Your home

EVERYONE IS ALLOWED to have a certain amount of tax-free income, and depending on your circumstances you may be entitled to more tax-free income than others.

Each of us, whatever our age and circumstances, is entitled to a personal allowance. For the 1997/98 tax year this is £4,045. If you are aged 65 or older, you may be entitled to a higher allowance, depending on your income (see page 42). There are three extra allowances that married couples, people looking after children on their own, blind people and widows can claim:

> **EXAMPLE**
> If you get married on 8 June you will have been married for ten months by the end of the tax year, and so you'll be entitled to ten-twelfths of the allowance. For the 1997/98 tax year the calculation is 10/12 x £1,830 = £1,525. Tax relief on this is £228.75.

Married couple's allowance
This allowance is £1,830 for the 1997/98 tax year, but the tax relief is restricted to 15%. So the tax saving is £274·50 a year, which works out at around £23 a month. You are entitled to a proportion of the allowance in the tax year in which you get married, calculated according to the number of months that you are married. If you get married between 6 April and 6 May, you are entitled to the full allowance, and after that you get the relevant number of twelfths.

You may be entitled to a higher married couple's allowance if you or your spouse is 65 or older (see page 42).

Additional personal allowance
This allowance is £1,830 for the 1997/98 tax year, and relief is restricted to 15%. To claim this allowance you must have a child living with you for at least part of the year, be unmarried, separated or divorced, or a widow or widower. The child must be your own child, a step-child, or legally adopted child under 18, and you must look after the child at your own expense. If the child is over 16, he or she must be in full-time education or be training full-time for a trade or profession.

Bear in mind, you can have only one additional personal allowance, regardless of the number of children living with you who meet these requirements. A man who gets married can continue to claim the additional personal allowance for the tax year in which he gets married, rather than claim the married couple's allowance; this usually makes sense because of the way the married couple's allowance is apportioned according to when you marry. A woman claiming the additional personal allowance can continue to claim for the year in which she marries. After that year neither can claim the allowance, unless the wife is incapacitated for the whole year.

Widow's bereavement allowance
This allowance is £1,830 for the 1997/98 tax year, and relief is restricted to 15%. A widow can claim this allowance in the year in which her husband dies. You need to have lived with your husband for at least some of the time in that year to qualify. You can claim the allowance for the following tax year unless you remarry before the start of that tax year. There's no equivalent allowance for widowers.

Blind person's allowance
This allowance is £1,280 for the 1997/98 tax year, and is not restricted. It is given to people who are registered blind with a local authority in England and Wales. Scotland and Northern Ireland do not have registers – the person must be unable to perform any work for which eyesight is essential.

MARRIAGE
Once you've got married you'll discover that the married couple's allowance is not the only thing that has an impact on your tax

> Independent financial adviser and *Moneywise* Ask the Professionals panellist Rebekah Kearey says:
>
> "Married couples should always look to redistribute their assets and investments between themselves so that as little tax is paid as possible. For example, a non-tax-paying spouse should own the unit trusts so that tax can be reclaimed on dividends. The higher-rate taxpayer would benefit more from PEPs since they have more tax to save. Assets can be moved between spouses so that both can use their capital gains tax thresholds."

position. You may be able to transfer some allowances between each other, you can transfer assets to each other without having to pay tax, and when you die, anything left to your spouse will not be liable for inheritance tax (IHT).

Allowances
Married couples aren't permitted to transfer their personal allowances unless the husband's income was lower than the personal allowance in the 1990/91 tax year, when rules changed so that husbands and wives are taxed separately. If you were eligible for the transitional allowance in the 1990/91 tax year, and every year since then, you may then be allowed to transfer some of the allowance.

You can transfer the blind person's allowance if the person entitled to it doesn't have enough income to make use of some or all of the allowance. You need to complete form 575 and the Inland Revenue will estimate the amount to be transferred. This will be done on a provisional basis and checked after the end of the tax year. If the amount was too low, a rebate will be paid, and if it was too high, the person to whom the allowance was transferred will have to pay back the tax. This may be done through the PAYE system.

Investments
If you have joint investments or savings accounts, the Inland Revenue will automatically treat them as if they were owned by each of you in equal shares, and tax each of you accordingly. If, in fact, you own the investments in different proportions, you are entitled to ask for the income to be taxed to reflect this; you need to make a joint declaration on form 17 giving details of the split between you. You can't, however, choose the proportions that suit you – you can only use the real shares. If you want to get income in certain proportions it would be better to have investments in your individual names.

Death

Your spouse will not be liable for any IHT on anything you leave to him or her (see Chapter 9).

SEPARATION AND DIVORCE

Although tax may be the last thing on your mind at such a time, you should tell your tax office that you and your spouse have separated. In the year you separate you will each continue to receive the amount of the married couple's allowance you were getting at the time you separated.

If you have a child living with you, you may be able to claim the additional personal allowance (see page 38) but not if you are receiving the full married couple's allowance. If you are getting half of the married couple's allowance, you may be entitled to part of the additional personal allowance to take the amount up to the full married couple's allowance. The married couple's allowance and the additional personal allowance are the same amount for the 1997/98 tax year (see pages 37 and 38).

Separation and divorce have an impact on your tax position because your living arrangements change and because there are special rules for maintenance payments. Once you have separated or divorced, you will each have a home. Unless you took out a mortgage together before July 1988, you will have been getting mortgage interest relief on £30,000; once you are apart, you will each be entitled to relief on the interest on £30,000 for your separate homes. If you took out a joint mortgage before July 1988, you will each have been getting relief on £30,000 to buy your home.

If you are paying your ex-spouse's mortgage interest, it's best to increase the maintenance you pay to include the relevant amount – then your spouse will actually pay the interest and benefit from the relief. That way you can still get the benefit of relief if you have a mortgage of your own.

There are no special tax rules for any voluntary maintenance payments you make or receive. Two sets of tax rules apply to legally enforceable maintenance payments, according to when the court order was made. Under the 'new' rules, if you make maintenance payments under a court order applied for after 15 March 1988, you get tax relief on up to £1,830 in 1997/98 – the amount is set in the Budget each year. This is called the maintenance deduction, and relief is restricted to 15%. You can't have the relief if the payment is directly to a child. However many people you pay maintenance to, the total amount of tax relief is the same. If your ex-spouse remarries, you'll no longer be entitled to the tax relief.

The 'old' rules apply to maintenance payments made under a court order applied for and agreements made before 15 March 1988, and in place by 30 June 1988. The tax relief you get is limited to the amount on which you received tax relief in the 1988/89 tax year. You can opt to switch to the new rules if it means that you would get more tax relief. Bear in mind that if you do switch, there is no tax relief on payments made directly to children, to someone other than your ex-husband or ex-wife, or to an ex-spouse who has remarried. To switch you need to complete form 142 – you can do this from before the start of the tax year up to 12 months after the end of the tax year for which you want the election to apply. And you must write to the person to whom you pay maintenance to inform them within 30 days of making the election. Once you have made the election you cannot withdraw it.

If you receive maintenance under the new rules, there is no tax to pay. Under the old rules, any payments you receive from your ex-husband or ex-wife are free of tax up to the amount of the married couple's allowance (£1,830 in 1997/98); anything above this amount is added to your other income in the usual way. This exemption is withdrawn if you remarry.

CHILDREN

Children have a personal allowance, so if their income exceeds this they will have to pay tax just like adults. Interest on savings accounts is usually paid with tax of 20% deducted. It is unlikely that your child is a taxpayer, so he or she should complete form R85 (from your bank or building society) so the interest can be paid without tax deducted. Otherwise, your son or daughter will have to reclaim the tax.

If a child's income is from investments given by their parents, it is the parents who may have to pay tax – the information must be included along with their own investment income on their tax returns. If the child's income from these investments is less than £100, they will not have to pay tax.

If your employer provides a nursery or playscheme which your child attends, you don't have to pay tax on the value of the child's place as long as your employer has satisfied certain conditions – your employer will be able to tell you what the position is. If you get help with childcare costs from your employer, you will pay tax; see page 53 for more on benefits provided by employers.

In later years

You may be entitled to a higher personal allowance and married couple's allowance if you were aged 64 or older before the beginning of the tax year; the amount to which you're entitled depends on your income. The higher personal allowance for those aged 65 to 74 is up to £5,220, and for those aged 75 and older it is up to £5,400. The married couple's allowance can be up to £3,185 if one of you was between 64 and 73 before the start of this tax year, and up to £3,225 if 74 or more. It's restricted to 15% in the usual way.

The higher allowances are reduced if your total income is at least £15,600. The extra allowance will be reduced by £1 for every £2 by which your income exceeds £15,600, but the allowances won't be reduced below the usual levels. As a guide, if your total income exceeds £17,950 you'll get only the usual allowances if you're between 65 and 74; if you're 75 or older the break-even level is £18,310.

Your 'total income' is any income you have less certain outgoings. If you receive income which has had tax deducted you need to include the gross amount. Deductions include pension contributions, donations to charity under Gift Aid or the payroll-giving scheme (see Chapter 2), and maintenance payments which get tax relief.

If your income exceeds £15,600 by only a small amount, it could be worth reorganising your finances to keep below the limit, even though this may seem an odd thing to

---

Independent financial adviser and *Moneywise* Ask the Professionals panellist Rebekah Kearey says:

"From the tax year in which you reach your 65th birthday, you become potentially eligible to enhanced personal and married couple's allowances. You can have the total additional allowance only if your income is below a threshold, currently £15,600. You lose £1 for every £2 by which your income exceeds the amount. If you are married and one of you has less income than this but the other is nearing this level of income, it is very important to ensure that income-generating savings and investments are transferred to the other spouse."

> **EXAMPLE**
> If you are aged 72, you could be entitled to a personal allowance of up to £5,220. Your total income is £16,000, so it exceeds the limit by £400 (£16,000 less £15,600), so the allowance is reduced by half of £400, which is £200. The allowance is therefore £5,020.

do. It can be done by opting for investments that provide a tax-free income (see Chapter 6). And for how pension income is taxed see Chapter 7.

If you are planning to retire abroad there are various tax-planning issues involved. If you have assets you plan to sell to fund your life abroad, bear in mind that this could give rise to a capital gains tax (CGT) bill. If you can, it's worth waiting until you've moved and are regarded as not resident in the UK for tax purposes because you won't then be liable to CGT. The Inland Revenue will regard you as non-resident from the date you leave, but only provisionally: it does not become 'official' until you've been overseas for a full tax year. The benefits of a personal pension can be paid to you abroad without deduction of UK tax if you're non-resident, but there may be local tax to pay.

BENEFITS

If you receive any social security benefits, you may need to check whether there's any tax to pay on them, as some benefits are taxable. If benefits are your only source of income in a tax year you will not need to worry about tax as your income won't be more than your personal allowance(s). But there will be income tax to pay if your income, including taxable benefits, comes to more than your personal allowances.

The following benefits are taxable:
- Jobseekers allowance.
- Income support paid because you are unemployed or on strike.
- Invalid care allowance and invalidity addition paid with a retirement pension.
- Job release allowance.
- Maternity pay.
- Incapacity benefit after 28 weeks.
- State pension.
- Statutory sick pay.
- Supplementary allowance paid when you are unemployed or on strike.
- Widowed mother's allowance and widow's allowance.

The following benefits are not taxable:
- Attendance allowance.
- Family credit.
- Income support paid for reasons other than unemployment, strikes, temporary layoffs or short-time working.
- Mobility allowance.
- War widows pension and widows payment.
- Child benefit, child's special allowance and guardian's allowance.
- Child dependency addition paid with taxable social security allowances and pensions.

Most benefits are paid without tax deducted. If you are working, any tax on benefits will be collected through PAYE (see Chapter 5). Otherwise, you will be sent a statement of how much you owe.

Your home

BUYING YOUR HOME is a financial transaction where the Inland Revenue knocks a little off your tax bill. In effect you get a discount on the interest you have to pay on a mortgage. The value of this relief has been eroded over the last few years; some expected Chancellor of the Exchequer, Gordon Brown, to announce its abolition in his first Budget in July 1997 – he didn't get rid of it but he has reduced it further.

For 1997/98 you get 15% tax relief on the part of your interest payment that relates to £30,000 of your mortgage (this will go down to 10% from April 1998). You are entitled to this relief even if you're a non-taxpayer. The relief is given only on loans for buying your only or main residence – this can be a house, flat, caravan or houseboat. You'll probably still be eligible for tax relief if you have to move away from your home temporarily because of your job, as long as you are away for less than four years and you expect to live in your home

> **EXAMPLE**
> If you take out an interest-only mortgage of £60,000 at a rate of 7%, your monthly payments are as follows:
> £30,000 x 7% x 85%, which is £1,785
> £30,000 x 7%, which is £2,100
> Total annual interest is £1,785 + £2,100 = £3,885
> Divided by 12 =£323.75. So, the tax relief is worth £26.25 a month.

again when you return. You should also get relief if you have to live in accommodation which goes with your job, but buy a home in which to live in the future. It is best to double check with your tax office as this can depend on individual circumstances.

If you own more than one property, you can't choose the one you want to get the relief on – it has to be the one you live in most of the time.

You may get the relief from your mortgage lender by paying the lower amount of interest; this means your mortgage is within the MIRAS scheme (MIRAS stands for mortgage interest relief at source). You fill in a form (MIRAS 70 or MIRAS 76) on taking out your mortgage which gives your lender the authority to ask you to pay the reduced amount of interest. Most lenders operate MIRAS, but you can pay the interest in full and let your tax office then adjust the amount of tax you pay on your income. To do this you complete form MIRAS 3.

Your loan may have to be outside MIRAS if it is for 'mixed purposes', for example. This is where money is borrowed partly to buy a home and partly for something else; only the part relating to home purchase qualifies for interest relief. The lender may be able to structure the loan in such a way that the relevant part can be in MIRAS.

There are some occasions when you can get tax relief on more than the interest on £30,000. Before July 1988, the £30,000 limit applied to each individual, but since then it has applied to the property. So if you bought a property with someone else before 1988 and are benefiting from relief on the interest on more than £30,000, bear in mind that you'll lose some tax relief if you remortgage.

If you are unable to sell your home but move anyway, you may be entitled to tax relief on the original mortgage for up to 12 months after you move. You'll still be entitled to the usual relief on your new mortgage. Your tax office can extend the 12-month period if you have particular problems in selling your old home.

If your mortgage is in joint names with someone else, you are treated as paying the interest equally. If you are a married couple you can elect to share the tax relief in any way you want, even if the loan is in the name of only one of you. You do this by making an 'allocation of interest election'. If the loan is in MIRAS – in other words, the tax relief is given automatically – making the election won't alter the level of relief you get as a couple. But if the loan isn't in MIRAS, and one of you is a non-taxpayer, making the election could make sense. You need to complete form 15 and send it to the Inland Revenue less than 12 months after the end of the tax year to which you want the allocation to apply. This will stay in force until you inform the Inland Revenue otherwise. You must both sign the form.

You need to tell your tax office of any changes in your circumstances which could affect your tax position; if you move out and let your home, for example, your mortgage will have to come out of MIRAS and the interest payments are set against the rent you receive when working out the tax you'll owe on the rent.

STAMP DUTY

Stamp duty is a tax you have to pay when you buy a house costing £60,000 or more; if the sale price is between £60,000 and £250,000 you pay 1% of the total sale price. In the July 1997 Budget, two new levels were introduced; stamp duty will be charged at 1·5% of the sale price if it is more than £250,000, and at 2% if it costs £500,000 or more. If you buy a leasehold flat, the stamp duty you pay depends on the ground rent.

LETTING YOUR HOME

If you let part of your home, some of any rental income may be tax free. If you have a lodger – someone who pays to live in your home, normally with meals provided and sharing the living rooms – you can opt to be in the rent-a-room scheme, under which the first £4,250 (in the 1997/98 tax year) of rental income can be tax free. So, if the income you get is less than £4,250, there's no tax to pay, and if you don't get a tax return, you don't need to tell the Inland Revenue about the income. If you do get a tax return, there's a box you need to tick to confirm you're in the scheme. If you let your home with another person, you each have a limit of £2,125 – if there are more than two of you, you each still have a limit of £2,125.

> **EXAMPLE**
> If you let a room for £150 a week, your rental income is £7,800. Under the rent-a-room scheme you'd pay tax on £7,800 a year, less £4,250, which is £3,550. If your expenses related to letting the room are £2,000, you'd pay tax on £7,800 less £2,000, which is £5,800, so you'd clearly be better off using the rent-a-room scheme.

Letting your home can be counted as a business and taxed accordingly – you can deduct certain expenses to arrive at the taxable figure. If the rent is more than £4,250 you can choose between paying tax on the amount of rent over £4,250, or paying tax as if it were a business.

Even if you opt for the rent-a-room scheme, you can change to the other system if it makes sense as long as you let your tax office know within one year of the end of the relevant tax year. You might want to do this if you make a loss, as you can then set this against other income to cut your tax bill. If you opt to have your profit taxed, this is added to your other taxable income and the rate of tax depends on all your taxable income.

Broadly speaking, you can claim most expenses you incur wholly and exclusively as a result of letting the property (though not capital expenses – see below). And you can claim an appropriate proportion of expenses that do not fit the wholly and exclusively description. If you are in doubt about a particular item of expenditure, consult your tax office. The following are typical expenses:

- Interest on a loan to buy or improve the property.
- Ground rent and other rent you pay for the property (if you don't own it).
- Gas, electricity, water rates.
- Council tax that you have to pay.
- Insurance.
- The cost of advertising for tenants.
- Fees to estate or accommodation agencies.
- Payments you make to someone to look after the keys and do the cleaning or gardening.
- Accountants' fees and solicitors' bills.
- The cost of maintenance, repairs, and redecoration (but not the cost of improvements).
- Furniture and so on if you let furnished accommodation: either you claim the cost of anything you replace (such as furniture, fridges, household linen and crockery) or you claim 10% (each year) of the net rent you receive – the net rent making a deduction for any bills such as water rates and council tax which are paid by you out of the rent but which could equally be paid directly by your tenant. You have to choose one basis or the other and stick to it.

If you let out only part of a property, or the property is let (or available for letting) for only part of the year, you will be able to claim an appropriate proportion of the expenses you incur.

Some expenditure counts as capital expenditure. The cost of buying a property is capital expenditure and you cannot claim any allowance for this; nor can you claim for alterations and improvements. You may be able to claim some of your expenditure if an improvement removed the need to carry out routine repairs, though you cannot claim the cost of extensive repairs that have to be carried out before you start to let the property. Routine repairs are an expense that can be deducted from the rent.

> Independent mortgage adviser and *Moneywise* Ask the Professionals panellist Walter Avrili says:
>
> "Because there are a number of tax implications when you decide to let part of your home or buy a property to let, not least for your mortgage, it is always best to get some advice for your particular circumstances."

It's quite possible to make a loss on your property; for example, you may have taken out a loan to buy the property and the interest on the loan plus other expenses may come to more than the rent you receive.

If you let out more than one property in the UK, you can pool all the expenses and deduct them from all the rental income before working out your taxable profit. If you let property abroad, you need to work out the profit separately; for example, if your expenses on property abroad exceed the rent, you can't deduct the extra expenses from the rental income you receive from your UK property.

You have made a loss if expenses exceed the income you have received. Losses on UK property can be set against rental income from UK property in future years, provided your rental business is continuous; if the business stops and starts again you won't be able to carry forward losses to the new business. Similarly, losses on property abroad can be set against rental income on foreign property in future years.

WORKING AT HOME

If you're employed and work at home you may be able to reduce your taxable income by deducting part of the costs: heating, lighting, telephone, and so on. If you rent your home and use part of it only for work, you may be able to deduct part of the rent. However, you'll only be able to make any of these deductions if you have to work at home. Using part of your home for work may mean you will have to pay CGT when you sell your home (see Chapter 8).

If you're self-employed and work at home, part of the costs of running your home can be treated as allowable expenses. Again, you'll lose some of your CGT exemption, but if you use the proceeds from selling your home to buy a property where you continue to work (even if it is a different kind of work), you won't have to pay CGT.

Action plan

- Check you are getting all the personal allowances to which you are entitled.

- If you're married and you want to keep your joint tax bill down, remember to ensure that you use up all your allowances and reorganise investments if necessary.

- If you separate from your husband or wife, or you get divorced, tell your tax office.

- If you pay or receive maintenance payments, check with your tax office that the tax treatment is right.

- If you have children make sure that they complete form R85 for any savings accounts they have the interest can then be paid without tax being deducted.

- If you're over 65, make sure the Inland Revenue knows and that you get any higher allowances to which you may be entitled.

- If you're over 65 and your income is at or near the total income limit for higher allowances (£15,600), work out whether you'd be better off rearranging your finances in order to let you keep more of the higher allowances.

- If you're considering letting your home, work out whether you should use the rent-a-room scheme.

TAX

5 Work

Whether you work for an employer, for yourself, or both, there are quite complex rules dictating how much of your cash you can keep. If you're employed your pay arrives with tax already taken off. Are you sure the right amount has been deducted? If you're self-employed, do you know which expenses you can deduct from your profits before working out your tax bill?

If you're employed

MOST OF US are aware that our pay comes to us with tax already deducted, according to our PAYE (pay as you earn) code, which represents the allowances to which we are entitled (see below).

The Inland Revenue provides employers with tables so they can work out how much tax to deduct. The Inland Revenue sends you

L You get the basic personal allowance.

H You get the basic personal allowance and either the additional personal allowance or the married couple's allowance.

P You get the whole of the higher personal allowance for people aged between 65 and 74.

V You get the whole of the higher married couple's allowance for people aged between 65 and 74.

K The deductions from your tax-free pay exceed your personal allowances.

NT You don't have to pay any tax on your income.

BR You might get this code if it relates to a second job – it means all your earnings from this source are taxed at the basic rate, and your allowances have been taken into account somewhere else.

DO All your earnings from this source are taxed at the higher rate.

OT Your deductions exceed the allowances to which you're entitled.

a notice of coding. The number in the code tells your employer how much tax-free pay you're allowed in the tax year; this is worked out using the allowances to which you're entitled and any tax relief you're due – an amount will also be deducted for any taxable perks (covered later in this chapter). The last digit of the result of this calculation is taken off and a letter is added which reflects the allowances to which you're entitled. (See box on page 51.)

The digit taken off is always assumed to be a nine, and you get one-twelfth of the resulting amount in tax-free pay each month. So, if your code is 404L, you get tax-free pay of one-twelfth of £4,049 a month, which is about £338.

> Tax expert and *Moneywise* Ask the Professionals panellist Janet Adam says:
>
> "Try and make sure your code number is correct so that the right amount of tax is deducted from your salary during the year. Otherwise you may end up with a substantial underpayment (or overpayment) of tax. Then you'd need to complete a tax return to ensure you comply with the law and pay the correct amount of tax."

Your allowances will be shown on the left-hand side of the notice of coding. Outgoings on which you're entitled to tax relief may also appear on this side of the notice, and may include contributions to a pension, or mortgage payments where the loan is not in the MIRAS scheme (see Chapter 4). On the right-hand side, there'll be a list of those things which are taxable on top of your pay, which'll reduce the amount of tax-free pay you receive; these may include perks, other earnings not taxed through PAYE, or maintenance payments received.

If you owe tax from a previous tax year which you have agreed with the Inland Revenue to pay in instalments, this will appear on the right-hand side too, as tax underpaid. If you are a higher-rate taxpayer and owe extra tax on investments (see Chapter 6), this will also be shown here. The married couple's allowance, additional personal allowance and widow's bereavement allowance are given at only 15% (see Chapter 4). In order for this to happen an allowance restriction will appear on the right-hand side of your notice.

If your taxable perks and other income are greater than your allowances, the code will begin with the letter K – this means the amount must be added to your salary and be taxed.

When you start your first job, your employer will give you form P46 to complete. This is sent to the Inland Revenue, and your employer will give you your PAYE code based on the personal allowance until the Inland Revenue informs your employer it should be changed. If you had claimed unemployment benefit or income support before starting the job, your benefit office will give you form P45, which you give to your employer.

You should be given form P45 when you leave your job – this will show your PAYE code, how much you've earned and how much tax you've paid since the start of the tax year. If you're not going to another job, but will be claiming benefits, you should give the P45 to your benefit office.

Perks

You have to pay tax on any perk you receive – benefit in kind – if you earn £8,500 or more, or are a director. The test is, normally, if you earn 'at a rate of £8,500' a year, so if you were paid at least £4,250 for six months' work or £2,125 for three months' work you'd be liable for tax on perks. In fact, you have to include the taxable value of any perks to work out whether you earn more than the minimum; and you have to add all your earnings from different jobs together.

A company director who earns less than £8,500 won't come into the net for tax on perks if he or she owns or controls no more than 5% of the shares in the company, is a full-time working director of the company, or works for a charity or non profit-making company and is not a director of an associated company.

Perks which are tax-free include:
○ Clothes specifically for your job – for example overalls.
○ Company vans heavier than 3·5 tonnes.

> **Example**
> If the list price plus extras of your 1,600 cc company car is £10,000, you do between 2,500 and 17,999 business miles, and your employer pays for your petrol, the tax you'll pay is worked out as follows: 35% of £10,000 is £3,500, and two-thirds of this is £2,333 – this is the taxable benefit for the car. The fuel benefit for this engine size is £740. So, £2,333 plus £740, which is £3,073, is added to your taxable income.

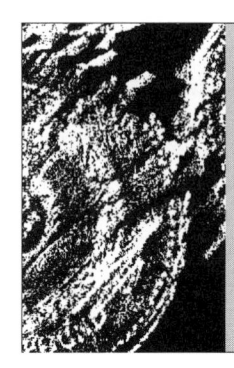

TAXABLE FUEL BENEFIT 1997/98

Cylinder capacity	Petrol	Diesel
1,400cc or less	£800	£740
Between 1,400cc and 2,000cc	£1,010	£740
More than 2,000cc	£1,490	£940

For cars without recognised cylinder capacity, the taxable benefit is £1,490.

- Discounts on goods and services.
- Life insurance.
- Pension contributions.
- Transport between home and work for the disabled who are unable to use public transport.
- Travelling or subsistence allowance when public transport is disrupted by industrial action.

Below we will look at three types of taxable perk in detail, and on page 58 there is a checklist of other potentially taxable perks.

Company cars

If your employer provides you with a private car, the tax you pay is based on 35% of the price of the car. The price used is the list price plus accessories and delivery charge, VAT and car tax where appropriate; this is subject to an upper limit of £80,000. The taxable benefit may be reduced according to the number of business miles you do in a tax year; if you do between 2,500 and 17,999 miles it is reduced by a third, if you do more than 18,000 miles it is reduced by two-thirds. It will be reduced by a further third if the car is four or more years old at the end of the tax year.

If your employer pays for your petrol as well, the taxable amount depends on your engine size.

Tax expert and *Moneywise* Ask the Professionals panellist Janet Adam says:

"If you have a cash alternative to a company car you need to do your sums carefully, taking into account the interest cost of the capital needed to buy a new car yourself, the number of business miles you can anticipate in a full year, and the mileage allowance your employer is prepared to pay you if you use your own car for business. Remember, you will need to insure your car for business use, which may be slightly more expensive."

Company car calculator

Should you go for a company car or stick with your own? This table shows you the average cost of a company car* compared with the cost of using your own.

COMPANY CAR COSTS

List price of company car	£14,875			
Car benefit less than 2,500 miles	35% of list price			
Car benefit 2,500–17,999 miles	23% of list price			
Car benefit more than 17,999 miles	12% of list price			
Marginal tax rate	40%			
Business miles per year	2,000	5,000	10,000	20,000
Car benefit	£5,206	£3,421	£3,421	£1,785
Fuel benefit	£890	£890	£890	£890
Total car benefit per year	£6,096	£4,311	£4,311	£2,675
Tax per year at 40%	£2,438	£1,724	£1,724	£1,070

OWN CAR COSTS

AA annual fee	£66			
Insurance fee	£365			
Road tax	£150			
Depreciation per 10,000 miles	£1,953			
Petrol costs per mile	8.5p			
Service and rrepair costs per mile	5.4p			
Marginal tax rate	40%			
Car allowance per year	£3,600			
Mileage allowance 4,000m	43p			
Mileage allowance 4,000m+	23p			
Private miles per year	5,000	5,000	5,000	5,000
Business miles per year	2,000	5,000	10,000	20,000
Mileage allowance per year	£860	£1,950	£3,100	£5,400
Total allowances	£4,460	£5,550	£6,700	£9,000
Tax per year on car allowance at 40%	£1,440	£1,441	£1,440	£1,440
Total car expenses per year	£1,544	£1,961	£2,656	£4,056
Total depreciation per year	£1,367	£1,953	£2,929	£4,882
Total cost per year	£4,351	£5,354	£7,025	£10,378
Minus car allowance per year	£3,600	-£3,600	-£3,600	-£3,600
ACTUAL COST PER YEAR	£751	£1,754	£3,425	£6,778
ADVANTAGE OF COMPANY CAR	-£1,687	£30	£1,701	£5,708

*All costs are based on average AA figures for a petrol car with a 1,600cc to 2,000cc engine.

Cheap loans

If you have a loan from your employer on which you pay little or no interest there may be tax to pay. Some loans qualify for tax relief anyway, and this affects the taxable value as a perk. If the loan from your employer qualifies for tax relief, you pay tax on the amount of interest you would have had to pay if you didn't get the cheap loan less the interest you pay your employer. The interest you would have had to pay is worked out using the official rate of interest, which was 6·75% as this book was published. If it is an interest-free loan, you are not allowed to deduct anything.

This amount is added to your taxable income and tax is charged at your top rate. But you still get tax relief on this.

If you get a cheap loan from your employer which wouldn't normally qualify for tax relief, it is tax free unless you earn £8,500 or more and the total of all cheap or interest-free loans from your employer which do not qualify for tax relief comes to more than £5,000. If your loans exceed the limit, you must pay tax on the difference between the interest you actually pay and the interest you would have paid if you had been charged the official rate of interest on all your loans.

> **EXAMPLE**
> If you get a cheap mortgage of £60,000 on which you pay interest at 4%, you work out the taxable value as follows. First deduct 4% of £60,000 from 6·75% of £60,000. This gives £1,650. Tax at 23% on this is £379·50. Then you can deduct an amount to reflect the tax relief to which you're entitled; this is 15% of £2,025 (the interest at 6·75% on £30,000, the limit for mortgage tax relief). So you take £303·75 from £379·50 and your tax bill for the cheap loan is £75·75.

Share schemes

Your employer may offer one of several types of scheme which give you shares in the company. Some share schemes have tax advantages as long as they meet certain conditions laid down by the Inland Revenue. The rules are quite complicated, and so is the section for these on your tax return (see Chapter 10).

- *Company share option plans*: For your shares to be tax free the maximum value of options per employee is £20,000 and the exercise price of the options must not be at a discount to the market price of the shares.
- *Profit-sharing schemes*: With an approved scheme you can be given up to £3,000-worth of shares, or 10% of earnings tax

free, whichever is higher, with an overall limit of £8,000 a year. To be approved the shares must be held in trust and not actually given to you for at least two years. However, this rule doesn't apply if your circumstances change, for example if you retire or are made redundant.

○ *Savings-related share option schemes*: Your employer can run a savings scheme giving you the option to buy its shares some years in the future at a price fixed now. You won't have to pay when the option is given to you or when you buy them. The price you pay for them must not be less than 80% of their market value at the time the option is given, but there may be capital gains tax (CGT) to pay when you sell or give away the shares. The maximum saving is £250 a month.

○ *Share option schemes*: With a share option scheme you are given the right to buy shares in your employer's company at a specific date in the future at today's market price. There's no tax to pay when you exercise your option if the scheme is an approved one and you were given the options before 17 July 1995, but any gain you make when you sell the shares or give them away will be liable to CGT (see Chapter 8).

If the scheme you are in is not approved, or your rights were granted on or after 17 July 1995, you'll pay income tax on the difference between market value when you exercise your option and the cost to you of shares, including any amount paid for the option. And there might be CGT to pay when you sell or give away your shares. This would be worked out using the difference between their market value when you exercise your option and their value at the time you dispose of them.

You'll see later in Chapter 10 that there are 'supplementary pages' for share chemes with separate sections for different types. And at first sight you might feel that completing them looks quite complicated. Working sheets are provided that help you establish the taxable amounts. Your employer should be able to provide the help you need in filling in this part of the tax return.

Checklist of potentially taxable perks

ACCOMMODATION
If accommodation is provided it's tax free, otherwise you pay tax on the amount your employer pays out less anything you contribute to these costs.

COMPANY VAN
If the van is less than four years old you pay tax on £500, and if it's more than four years old, you pay on £350.

CRÈCHE/DAY NURSERY
These are tax free, but if your employer pays cash for care or provides vouchers, these are taxable.

CREDIT CARDS AND CHARGE CARDS
These are taxed on the amount your employer pays out, less any contributions you make.

FEES AND SUBSCRIPTIONS
These are tax free as long as the organisation you pay these to is approved by the Inland Revenue and relevant to your job, otherwise you're taxed on the cost to your employer.

FOOD AND DRINK
These are tax free provided they are available for all employees.

GIFTS
Genuinely personal gifts are tax free, and other gifts you receive related to your job are tax free provided they cost no more than £150. If you're given something that was previously lent to you, this would be taxed on its taxable value (see above).

LUNCHEON VOUCHERS
15p per working day is tax-free.

PRIVATE MEDICAL INSURANCE
You pay tax on the cost to your employer.

MOBILE PHONES
You pay tax on £200.

RELOCATION AND REMOVAL EXPENSES
If you are transferred by your employer or have to move because of your job and your employer pays removal expenses, these are tax free up to £8,000.

SCHOLARSHIPS
If you're awarded a scholarship it will be tax free as long as you are enrolled for at least one academic year and attend full-time for an average of at least 20 weeks a year. The maximum is £7,000 or the amount of a grant from a public body, whichever is higher. If it's greater, the whole lot is taxable. Scholarships awarded by your employer to your children are taxable, unless the scholarship comes from a trust fund.

SEASON-TICKET LOANS
These are tax free as long as the total of cheap loans from your employer is no more than £5,000 (see above).

SUGGESTION SCHEMES
If you receive an award through your employer's suggestion scheme, this is tax free up to £5,000 overall.

WORKING ABROAD

The tax treatment of earnings from employment abroad depends on your 'residence' status. You will be regarded as non-resident for tax purposes if you are abroad for a complete tax year or more, throughout which time you work full-time outside the UK, and any visits you make to the UK average less than 91 days in a tax year. In this case you won't have to pay UK tax on your earnings abroad.

If you don't spend a whole tax year abroad, you'll still be resident and ordinarily resident in the UK, but you may still avoid UK tax on earnings from employment abroad if you spend at least 365 days abroad and acquire a 365-day qualifying period. If the 365 days abroad coincide with a complete tax year (from 6 April one year to 5 April the next) you should not have a problem, but if those 365 (or more) days straddle two tax years you may be able to claim the 'foreign earnings deduction', which basically means you won't have to pay tax on the money you have earned abroad.

If you return to the UK for a break at sometime during the qualifying period of 365 (or more) days, this may affect your entitlement to the deduction. First, if you spend more than 62 continuous days in the UK you won't be able to claim the deduction. If your visit (or visits) are for 62 days or fewer, you need to add up:
- The days you spent abroad both before and after coming back to the UK.
- The days you spent in the UK.

If the total comes to 365 (or more) days, and the number of days spent in the UK does not exceed one-sixth of the total, you have built up a qualifying period and can claim the foreign earnings deduction.

If you make more than one visit back home, the one-sixth rule applies to the total of all the days spent abroad and in the UK.

When you claim the foreign earnings deduction, you won't have to pay tax on the income earned from employment abroad. You will still be eligible for the usual UK tax allowances, including the personal allowance, and you will be able to use this for

> **EXAMPLE**
> You are employed abroad for 183 days (six months), and you come back to the UK for 30 days (one month). Then you return to your employment abroad for another 183 days. The total number of days comes to 183 + 30 + 183 = 396. One-sixth of 396 is 66. You spent much less than that – 30 days – in the UK and the total period is at least 365 days, so you can claim the foreign earnings deduction.

other income you might receive, such as the interest on a building society deposit account. Remember to claim back any tax deducted at source if you can then set it against your personal allowance.

Travel expenses paid by your employer to and from your job abroad are tax free. The same applies if your employer pays travel costs for your spouse and any children younger than 18. They can have two paid-for trips in any one tax year tax free, provided you are working abroad for at least 60 continuous days. If you pay these costs yourself, your own travel costs (but not those of your family) count as an allowable expense which can be deducted from the income you earn abroad before the tax is worked out (though there won't be any tax if you can claim the foreign earnings deduction).

If you're self-employed

EVEN IF YOU BELIEVE YOU'RE SELF-EMPLOYED, you may not be in the eyes of the Inland Revenue, which states that if you can answer yes to the following questions, you'll usually be regarded as self-employed for tax purposes:

- Do you have the final say in how the business is run?
- Do you risk your own money in the business?
- Are you responsible for meeting the losses as well as for taking the profits?
- Do you provide the main items of equipment that you need to do your job, not just the small tools many employees provide for themselves?
- Are you free to hire other people on your own terms to do the work you have taken on? Do you pay them out of your own pocket?
- Do you have to correct unsatisfactory work in your own time and at your own expense?

If you do most of your work for one company and you are paid without having to submit invoices, the Inland Revenue may decide you're employed rather than self-employed.

If you are self-employed, you are responsible for your own tax and National Insurance (covered later in this chapter), so once you

> Independent financial adviser and *Moneywise* Ask the Professionals panellist Kean Seager says:
>
> "There is no necessity to choose a particular year-end. In the old days the choice of year-end provided some tax advantages, but this is no longer the case. As a result you can choose any day in any month that you like. But with self assessment putting greater responsibility on the self-employed person, a year-end of 31 March is likely to be the favourite date as it keeps things as simple as possible."

become self-employed you must inform your tax office and the Contributions Agency of the DSS that you are in business, and you are responsible for telling the Inland Revenue about all your income. Once you have told the tax office that you are in business, you will probably be sent a tax return each year.

Because you are responsible for all of this, you need to keep full and accurate records of your business transactions. You pay tax on your annual profits, and you can choose the 12-month period you want to be your 'accounting year'. You can opt for it to coincide with the tax year – 6 April to 5 April – or to the end of particular month, possibly 12 months after you start trading. Your tax bill for a particular tax year will be based on your profits for the accounting year which ends in that tax year. So, for example, if your year-end date is 30 June, your tax bill for the 1998/99 tax year will be based on profits for the accounting year ending 30 June 1998.

There are special rules when you start working for yourself and when you stop:

- For the first year you are in business, you are taxed on the profits for the period from the date you started to the following 5 April.
- For the second year you are taxed on the profits of the 12 months to your accounting date in that year, providing that date falls 12 months or more after the date on which you started in business. If it doesn't, you'll be taxed on the profits of the first 12 months of your business.
- For the third year you are taxed on the profits for your accounting year ending in that year.

If this means that some of your profit is taxed more than once, you are entitled to an adjustment known as overlap relief when your business ends.

The way you are taxed for the tax year in which you stop working for yourself depends on when you started. If you started on or after 6 April 1994, you are taxed on your profits for the period from the end of the last accounting year to the date of closure. You can deduct overlap profit from this to calculate the amount you will pay tax on.

If you started in business before this and you close down in this tax year (1997/98) you could be taxed according to the rules described above, but, for various reasons, the Inland Revenue might decide you should be taxed according to the old rules. Under the old rules you pay tax according to whichever of the two following methods produces the higher tax bill:

- Your actual profits for the tax year and the old system of taxing on previous year's profits will apply to the years before then.
- Your actual profits for the last three years (tax years or accounting years).

If your business was established before 6 April 1994, you will have been taxed according to transitional rules as self assessment and the timing of tax payment described above were being introduced. Previously, if you were self-employed you would have paid tax for a specific tax year on the profits for your accounting year ending in the previous tax year. So if your year-end is 30 June you would have paid tax for the 1994/95 tax year on your profits to 30 June 1993.

For the 1996/97 tax year there are transitional rules. You pay tax on the average profit for the two years ending in the 1996/97 tax year, so if your year-end is 30 June you add together your taxable profits for the year ending 30 June 1995 and for the year ending 30 June 1996; divide this by two to arrive at the amount on which you pay tax. For 1997/98 you pay tax on your profit to 30 June 1997.

As explained in Chapter 3, you have to make two payments on account towards your tax bill each year: the first on 31 January and the second one on 31 July. If there is any further tax to pay, you need to pay it on 31 January in the following year. For 1997/98 the payments are based on your tax bill for the previous tax year 1996/97. If it turns out that you should have paid more than this, you'll pay the extra on 31 January 1999; if you shouldn't have paid as much, then you should receive your repayment on that date.

HOW TO WORK OUT YOUR TAXABLE PROFITS

Your profits for tax purposes will probably be slightly different to your 'real' profits, because not all expenses can be deducted under the tax rules, for example. So you might well work out your real profits first and then take into account certain expenses or deduct some things on which you get tax relief.

Allowable expenses

For an expense to be allowed it must be incurred 'wholly and exclusively' for the purpose of your business. If you work at home there will be some expenses which relate to both, so you can deduct only part of those expenses to calculate your taxable profit. You apportion these costs according to how much of the property you use for business and also in terms of the time it is used for business. The types of costs you can claim would include things such as goods or materials bought and sold or used, small tools and the running costs of vehicles.

Once you've deducted your allowable expenses you may be able to reduce your taxable profits further using capital allowances or other losses. It is important to be careful about these calculations as it is possible to waste allowances if you do not make deductions in a suitable order.

Capital allowances

If you've bought equipment you can't deduct the cost as an expense. But you can deduct part of the cost each year as a 'capital allowance'. You can deduct capital allowances for equipment, buildings, vehicles and patents. If you buy something which you use both privately and for your work, you can only deduct a suitable proportion.

In the year you buy something of this sort you can deduct 25% of the cost – however you paid for it – as a capital allowance. Anything you have in the way of equipment and so on is lumped together in a pool. In the years after you buy the item you can deduct 25% of the remaining value. So you simply deduct 25% of your pool each year as a capital allowance. If you sell something in your pool during the year, you deduct the proceeds up to the original cost of the item before working out your 25% allowance.

And if you sell an item for more than its written-down value, the difference is added to your profits – this is called a balancing charge; if you sell it for less, the difference is then deducted, which leaves a balancing allowance.

You may end up with several pools. Items which you use both for business and privately should be kept in a separate pool, and cars also have to be kept in a separate pool. You can also have a separate pool for items which you don't expect to keep for long; these are known as short-life assets, and may include computers which you expect to upgrade. So anything you think you'll dispose of within five years should be in one pool, but if in the end you keep something longer you can add it to your standard pool. You may be entitled to capital allowances for computer software if it has a useful life of more than two years.

Losses
There are several options for using losses for one tax year to reduce your tax bill for other years. If you make a loss in the first four years you are in business, you can set it against other income in the three years before the year in which you make the loss, starting with the earliest. If you want to do this you must make a claim within one year and ten months of the end of the tax year in which the loss was made. Losses made after this can be set against other income or gains for the same tax year, the previous tax year, or against future profits. To set a loss against income or gains for the same tax year or previous years, you must make the claim within one year and ten months of the end of the year in which you make the loss. To set a loss against future profits, you have five years and ten months after the end of the tax year for which you make a loss.

VAT
Another tax you may have to deal with when you work for yourself is value added tax (VAT). If your business is a certain size you have to register with Customs and Excise. VAT is one tax that is not administered by the Inland Revenue – if you ask your tax office for help, you'll be referred to Customs and Exercise. You may decide you want to register, even if it's not compulsory. Once registered you will be given a VAT number, and you can then charge VAT for your goods or services; you will also be paying VAT on certain goods or services you buy for business purposes. If you are registered you can deduct the VAT you pay from the VAT

you receive, and if you have paid more than you have received, Customs and Excise will send you a rebate; if you have received more than you have paid, you pay Customs and Excise.

It is compulsory to register for VAT if at the end of any month the value of your supplies in the last year on which you pay VAT is more than £48,000. You also have to register if you think it's likely that the taxable value of your supplies over the next 30 days will exceed £48,000. If you register you have to complete a VAT return every three months and send it to Customs and Excise. You also have to keep records for VAT purposes, so if you don't have to register you need to decide whether the money you may save is worth the extra work. If you do decide to register for VAT, the records you need to keep include:

- Business and accounting records.
- A VAT account that shows the amount of VAT you pay and the amount you receive.
- Copies of all VAT invoices you issue.
- All VAT invoices you receive.
- Documents relating to any imports or exports.
- Any debit notes or credits that alter your invoices.

It can be quite a complicated area, so contact Customs and Excise for more details (your local office will be in the telephone book).

National Insurance

ANYONE EARNING MORE than a certain amount has to pay National Insurance contributions on their income. Employers also have to pay National Insurance contributions on behalf of their employees. There are four types of contributions:

- **Class 1:** You pay these if you are employed. You pay 'primary' contributions and your employer pays 'secondary' contributions (see below).
- **Class 2:** You pay these if you are self-employed. It's a flat rate contribution of £6·15 a week in 1997/98, unless you earn less than £3,480 a year.
- **Class 3:** This is a voluntary contribution which you can choose to pay if you are not earning or have an interrupted

National Insurance contributions record. The rate for 1997/98 is £6·05 a week.
- **Class 4:** These contributions are also payable by the self-employed. If you have profits of between £7,010 and £24,180 in 1997/98 you are liable to pay Class 4 contributions of 6% of those profits.

Class 1 contributions depend on how much you earn, and whether or not you are 'contracted out' of the state earnings-related pension scheme – SERPS (see Chapter 7). They are also governed by 'middle band earnings'. Middle band earnings are your earnings between the 'lower earnings limit' and the 'upper earnings limit'. In 1997/98 the lower earnings limit is £62 a week (£3,224 a year); the upper earnings limit is £465 a week (£24,180 a year).

If you earn less than £62 a week you don't pay National Insurance contributions. If you earn more than £62 a week you pay contributions of:
- 2% of the first £62 a week.
- 10% of the middle band earnings between the lower and the upper earnings limits. This is reduced to 8.4% of middle band earnings if you are contracted out of SERPS (see Chapter 7).
- No contributions for salary earned above the upper earnings limit.

Employers also pay National Insurance contributions. Their contribution scale is more complicated, depending on the type of pension scheme used to contract out of SERPS. Unlike employee contributions, employers have to contribute in respect of all the salary earned, unless the employee earns less than £62 a week.

Although you pay contributions from your salary, there are circumstances when you are unable to work. In some cases you will receive National Insurance credits. These are when:
- You are still in full-time education between the ages of 16 and 18.
- You are on an approved training course (not university).
- You are claiming benefits such as unemployment benefit, maternity benefit or incapacity benefit.
- You are an unemployed man aged between 60 and 65.

If you are at home because you are looking after children or an elderly relative you qualify for home responsibilities protection. This reduces the total number of years you need to make NI contributions to qualify for a state pension. You automatically receive the protection if you are claiming child benefit but if you are looking after an elderly person you will need to notify your local Benefits Agency. The address will be in your local phone book.

You won't be building up a pension if you are at university, taking a career break or living abroad. You can make up for the lost years by paying Class 3 National Insurance contributions of £6·05 a week for the 1997/98 tax year. You are allowed to fill any gaps in your National Insurance record for the last six years.

Action plan

If you're employed:

❍ Check that your PAYE code is correct.

❍ If you have a choice between taking a company car or cash, follow our calculator to work out which option would leave you better off.

❍ Check which perks are taxable and which are not to make sure you know the position – and that the Inland Revenue are getting it right.

If you're self-employed:

❍ Make sure you understand the new responsibilities for record-keeping and paying tax under self assessment.

❍ Double check the allowable expenses and capital allowances you are using to work out your taxable profit.

❍ Use up losses – don't waste them.

❍ Consider registering for VAT.

TAX

6 Savings and investments

Tax on savings and investments can be payable at different rates, at different times, and for different reasons. Some of your investments can be taxed in two ways, others can be more tax-efficient, and many can be tax free.

You can even have two versions of the same investment and pay tax on one and not the other, depending on how you hold the investments. So before you put your money into a savings plan or investment, it's essential that you understand how much tax will be payable, and how you can reduce this tax. There are three types of tax that investments may be liable for:

- Income tax – on interest earned, on dividends, and on other income distributions.
- Capital gains tax (CGT) – on gains, or profits made, when an investment is sold or transferred.
- Inheritance tax (IHT) – on the value of investments gifted or left in an estate.

Income tax and CGT are the taxes that can most affect your investments; IHT is payable only by your heirs on investments you have already built up. In this chapter we explain how income tax and CGT are charged on all major UK investments, and how you can plan your finances to pay less tax. For more on IHT see Chapter 9.

By minimising the tax on your investments, you will maximise their performance. For example, over time, a low-tax or no-tax investment will always produce a higher return than an equivalent taxed investment. This is because with less tax deducted, compound interest builds up faster – you get tax free interest on tax-free interest. This is seen clearly when unit trusts are held tax free in a PEP: over 15 years to 1 July 1997, £1,000 in a UK equity income unit trust would have grown to £10,472, but £1,000 in the same unit trust held in a PEP would have grown to £12,998.

Tax-free and tax-efficient investments are therefore far more attractive than investments that are taxed. But remember that you should never put money into tax-free savings just because they are tax free! You must have proper financial planning reasons for choosing a tax-free investment: an investment must first suit your needs, in terms of risk and returns, and if it can be held tax free, then so much the better.

If you choose your investment solely on the basis of low taxation you could end up losing money. This is what happened to some investors in the late 1980s who put money into the former Business Expansion Scheme (BES) for maximum tax breaks. Many of the business ventures failed, and the investments were lost. A tax break on nothing is worth nothing. Tax breaks do differ, though, because different rates of tax apply to different investments. In other words, some investments are more tax free than others, so it's important to claim the tax breaks that are most beneficial to you, in your current circumstances. You might benefit most from investment returns that are free of income tax – for example from a PEP or certain National Savings plans. Or you may prefer to have tax relief on the money you pay in, for example through the Enterprise Investment Scheme (EIS). And you'll definitely want an investment that gives tax relief and grows free of all taxes, the only examples of which are employers pensions or personal pensions. For more on tax and pensions see Chapter 7, but for more on tax on all types of investments first look at the tax-efficient savings and investments flowchart on page 18, which allows you to work out the investments suitable for you and gives you an idea of the tax-efficient investments you can use. Then turn to the 'Tax on UK investments' listing, starting on page 71, which gives you all the information you need on how the investment works, what's on offer, and the returns you can expect.

Independent financial adviser and *Moneywise* Ask the Professionals panellist Brian Dennehy says:

"Tax benefits and flexibility need to be carefully weighed. For example, there's no doubt that pension contributions are very attractive because of the tax relief. But the other side of that coin is that 75% of your pension fund must be used to generate an income in retirement, which is also taxable. On the other hand, with a PEP you don't get tax relief on the contributions, but the income can be taken tax free, and you can cash in the whole PEP fund without restriction at any time. For most people the answer is a bit of both."

Tax on UK investments

ALL INVESTMENTS ARE, in theory, liable to either income tax or CGT on the returns they produce, but successive governments have granted tax-free status, special lower rates of tax, and other tax breaks to certain investments over certain periods.

They have done this to encourage you to put your money in particular types of investment. For example, in 1987 the then Conservative government introduced tax-free PEPs to let you hold shares with all dividend income and capital gains free of tax. A few years later it changed the rules to allow funds of shares, such as unit trusts and investment trusts, to be included in PEPs, to let you have lower-risk stockmarket investment tax-free, too. Then, in 1993, the government launched two new plans – the Enterprise Investment Scheme (EIS) and venture capital trusts (VCTs) – with tax relief and other tax breaks to increase investment in start-up companies.

So tax breaks on investment can have as much to do with overall government policy as they do with investors' needs, and this is why some of the more generous tax breaks are offered on the more risky – and less popular – investments. But there are still tax-efficient investments with much lower levels of risk, and it is the risk – and the return – that you should think about first. In order to help you do this we have divided the investments into four risk categories:

- Deposit-based savings (low risk).
- Fixed-interest securities (medium risk).
- Insurance-based investments (medium/higher risk).
- Stockmarket investments (high risk).

Once you have chosen the risk level that best suits you, compare the tax treatment of the appropriate investments and find the most tax-efficient way to save and invest. Tax-efficient savings and investments are indicated by this symbol: ✪

Deposit-based savings

CURRENT ACCOUNTS

Current accounts are offered by banks and building societies as a facility for holding, paying in and withdrawing cash. You pay money into the account and instruct the bank or building society to make payments on your behalf and pay cash to you on demand.

Cash can be withdrawn or paid in a number of different ways: cheque, debit card, standing order, direct debit mandate, or cash card. Current accounts are not considered to be investments, but most now pay a low rate of interest on credit balances, though this is generally a lower rate than the interest available on savings accounts and other deposit-based investments. And because interest is earned on your money, it is therefore taxable by the Inland Revenue.

Income tax: Tax is deducted from interest payments at the savings rate of 20%. Non-taxpayers can reclaim this tax or arrange for interest to be paid gross (at the bank or building society). Lower-rate and basic-rate taxpayers have no further tax to pay, but higher-rate taxpayers have extra to pay.

Capital gains tax: None.

SAVINGS ACCOUNTS

Savings accounts are offered by banks, building societies, and other deposit takers that pay interest on cash deposits. You can withdraw money on demand or by giving notice. Interest rates paid are higher than those on current accounts and are often tiered – the rate increases as you put more money in – but over the long term, the interest may not be enough to offset the effect of inflation on the buying power of your cash deposit. Interest on savings accounts is taxable.

Income tax: Tax is deducted from interest payments at the savings rate of 20%. Non-taxpayers can reclaim this tax or arrange for interest to be paid gross (at the bank or building society). Lower-rate and basic-rate taxpayers have no further tax to pay, but higher-rate taxpayers have extra to pay.

Capital gains tax: None.

Term accounts and bonds

Term accounts and bonds are lump-sum investments from banks and building societies that are designed to run for a set period of time, usually from one to five years. They either pay interest regularly or at the end of the term as a lump sum. Interest rates may be variable, or fixed for the duration of the term. If the rate is fixed, you risk losing out if rates on other investments rise. With some bonds you cannot get your money back before the end of the term, and so your money is effectively locked in for the term. With other bonds you can withdraw your money but there are interest penalties and/or notice periods, so it may be impossible or costly to get your money back quickly. Interest is taxable.

Income tax is deducted from interest payments at the savings rate of 20%. Non-taxpayers can reclaim this tax or arrange for interest to be paid gross (at the bank or building society). Lower-rate and basic-rate taxpayers have no further tax to pay. Higher-rate taxpayers have extra to pay.

Capital gains tax: None.

✪ Tax-exempt special savings accounts (TESSAs)

TESSAs are five-year bank or building society savings account which can pay interest on cash deposits with no tax deducted – provided the following special TESSAs rules are met:

❍ You can have only one TESSA at a time, though it is transferable from one bank or building society to another (though with penalties incurred).
❍ You can invest a maximum of £9,000 over the five years – up to £3,000 in year one, then up to £1,800 in each of the next four years, provided you do not exceed the overall limit of £9,000.
❍ You must leave the capital untouched for the full five years, but you can withdraw some of the interest that has been earned on your account balance without losing the tax breaks – the maximum amount you are allowed is the 'net' amount of interest (the amount you would have received if the account was not tax free).

You receive your capital and tax-free interest at the end of the five-year term. If, for any reason, you need to withdraw capital from your TESSA before then it loses its tax-free status, and all the interest accrued becomes taxable. However, even if you do this you will not usually be any worse off, as the net interest from a prematurely closed TESSA will usually be no lower than the rate on a standard, taxable savings account.

If you've invested the maximum allowed in a TESSA you can withdraw this money and decide to invest it elsewhere, or – thanks to a ruling in the 1994 Budget – roll-over the full £9,000 capital into a new TESSA. These are the roll-over rules:

- You can roll-over all of the capital from your first TESSA into a follow-on TESSA (but if you roll-over all of the capital, you can't roll-over any interest).
- You have six months from the date of maturity to roll-over the capital.
- Your original TESSA provider will issue a maturity certificate. If you take out a follow-on TESSA with a different provider, your original provider will send your certificate to your new provider.
- If you invest less than £9,000 in your follow-on TESSA, you can go on saving over the next four years, up to £1,800 each year, but total investment is capped at £9,000. So, if you invest £9,000 initially you cannot put any more money into a follow-on TESSA.
- Interest earned on an original TESSA can be reinvested in a follow-up TESSA provided you invested less than £3,000 over the original five-year term. You can then add to this interest to invest up to £3,000 in year one.
- Once you have opened a follow-on TESSA you have 12 months in which to invest your first-year maximum.
- Follow-on TESSAs must be held for another five years to qualify for tax-free interest.

If you do not tell your TESSA provider that you intend to roll-over the proceeds into a follow-on TESSA it will transfer the money into an ordinary account. Interest from then on will be taxable.

Some TESSAs require a 'feeder account' to be set up, holding the full £9,000, to qualify for the highest rates. Cash in the TESSA is tax free, but cash in a feeder account is subject to income tax.

Over the long term, tax-free TESSAs produce higher returns than equivalent taxable savings accounts, but do not pay as much as share-based investments and are eroded by inflation.

Income tax: Interest is tax free, but becomes taxable at the savings rate of 20% if you withdraw capital during the five-year term; this tax is due in the year of withdrawal. Interest equivalent to the interest net of 20% can be withdrawn during the term without losing overall tax-free status.

Capital gains tax: None

NATIONAL SAVINGS CAPITAL BONDS

National Savings Capital Bonds are savings bonds issued by the government and they pay a guaranteed rate of interest on cash deposits, which is taken at the end of five years. You can withdraw cash before the end of the five years, but you will incur penalties, and you could lose out if the interest rates on competing investments rise. Fixed interest is taxable and can be eroded by inflation.

Income tax: Interest is paid gross (without any tax deducted) but tax is payable at the savings rate of 20%. Higher-rate taxpayers have more tax to pay. Interest is not paid until the end of five years, but taxpayers are taxed on the interest each year as it is credited to the bond – via their tax returns – and may have to pay a tax bill each year. Non-taxpayers have no tax to pay.

Capital gains tax: None.

✪ NATIONAL SAVINGS CERTIFICATES

National Savings Certificates are five-year savings bonds producing a guaranteed tax-free rate of interest. Interest rates increase each year and are fixed for each year. At the end of the five-year term you can take your interest and capital, or reinvest in a new issue of certificates. You can withdraw cash before the end of the five years, but there are penalties, and you could lose out if interest rates on competing investments rise. Fixed interest can be eroded by inflation.

Income tax: Interest is tax free (and paid with no tax deducted).

Capital gains tax: None.

✪ NATIONAL SAVINGS CHILDREN'S BONUS BONDS

These are five-year tax-free savings bonds purchased by adults (older than 16 years) on behalf of children up to the age of 16 (a bond purchased for a 16-year-old would run until the child reaches 21). Interest is fixed for the five-year term. Fixed interest can be eroded by inflation, though, and you could lose out if interest rates on competing investments rise.

Income tax: Interest is tax free, even when bonds are bought by parents as a gift for children; investments bought for children are normally taxed as income of the parent.

Capital gains tax: None.

NATIONAL SAVINGS FIRST OPTION BONDS

National Savings FIRST Option Bonds are savings bonds that pay a fixed rate of interest for a year at a time. At the end of the year you have the option to reinvest for the following year at a new fixed rate, or to withdraw your capital and interest. You can continue reinvesting indefinitely.

Income tax: Tax is deducted from interest payments at the savings rate of 20%. Non-taxpayers can reclaim this tax. Lower-rate and basic-rate taxpayers have no further tax to pay, but higher-rate taxpayers have extra to pay.

Capital gains tax: None.

NATIONAL SAVINGS INCOME BONDS

National Savings Income Bonds are savings bonds that pay out interest on a monthly basis. Interest rates are variable and tiered, so your income can fall if interest rates generally fall. After the first year you can cash them in by giving three months' notice.

Income tax: Interest is paid gross (without any tax deducted) but tax is payable at the savings rate of 20%. Non-taxpayers have no tax to pay. Higher-rate taxpayers have more tax to pay.

Capital gains tax: None.

✪ NATIONAL SAVINGS INDEX-LINKED CERTIFICATES

National Savings Certificates are five-year savings bonds that produce a guaranteed tax-free rate of interest. Interest rates are fixed at a set number of percentage points above the rate of inflation, which is measured by the RPI; this ensures your investment is inflation proofed. At the end of the five-year term, you can take your interest and capital, or reinvest in a new issue of certificates.

You can withdraw cash before the end of the five years, but remember there are penalties.

Income tax: Interest is tax free, and paid with no tax deducted.

Capital gains tax: None.

NATIONAL SAVINGS INVESTMENT ACCOUNTS

National Savings Investment Accounts are savings accounts that pay a variable rate of interest on cash deposits. You have to give one month's notice of any withdrawals, so these accounts are the National Savings equivalent of bank or building society notice accounts. As with many savings accounts, the interest may not be enough to offset the effect of inflation on the buying power of your cash deposit. Interest is taxable.

Income tax: Interest is paid gross (without any tax being deducted) but tax is payable at the savings rate of 20%. Non-taxpayers have no tax to pay. Higher-rate taxpayers have more tax to pay.

Capital gains tax: None.

✪ NATIONAL SAVINGS ORDINARY ACCOUNTS

National Savings Ordinary Accounts are savings accounts that allow you to receive a certain amount of interest tax free. Interest rates are variable and usually low, so they may not be enough to offset the effect of inflation on the buying power of your cash deposit.

Income tax: £70 (£140 from a joint account) of interest a year is tax free. Interest over and above £70 (or £140) is paid out gross (without any tax deducted) but tax is payable at the savings rate of 20%. Non-taxpayers have no tax to pay. Higher-rate taxpayers have more tax to pay.

Capital gains tax: None.

NATIONAL SAVINGS PENSIONERS BONDS (GRANNY BONDS)

National Savings Pensioners Bonds are five-year bonds open only to people aged 60 or more; they pay a fixed rate of interest on a monthly basis. You can withdraw money before the end of the five-year term if you are able to give 60 days' notice and pay a penalty of 60 days' interest. Interest is fixed for the five-year term, but fixed interest can be eroded by inflation, and you could lose out if interest rates on competing investments rise. However, pensioners bonds traditionally pay more than most bank and building society savings accounts.

Income tax: Interest is paid gross (without any tax deducted) but tax is payable at the savings rate of 20%. Non-taxpayers have no tax to pay. Higher-rate taxpayers have more tax to pay.

Capital gains tax: None.

✪ NATIONAL SAVINGS PREMIUM BONDS

National Savings Premium Bonds are not savings bonds – they are an entitlement to take part in a government-approved prize draw. You pay in a lump sum of at least £100 to buy bonds, and the maximum holding is £20,000. No interest is paid to bondholders – the interest is used to produce a prize fund. Each bond stands a chance of winning a prize ranging anywhere from £50 up to £1m. You can have any prizes reinvested in further bonds or paid out to you tax free, and you get your capital back when you cash in the bonds.

Income tax: Premium Bonds prizes are tax free.

Capital gains tax: None.

Fixed-interest investments

GILTS (BRITISH GOVERNMENT STOCK)

Gilts are loans from you to the government, for which you are paid interest at a fixed rate (known as the coupon). Interest is paid at this rate twice a year for the lifetime of the gilt. Gilts are traded on the stockmarket in units of £100 (known as the nominal value), but the price of a gilt can be more or less than this depending on the fixed rate of interest it offers, so it is possible to buy and sell gilts and make a capital gain. Or you can buy gilts and hold them to redemption, when you will get the nominal value back.

Income tax: Tax is deducted from the interest payments at the savings rate of 20%. Non-taxpayers can reclaim the tax. Higher-rate taxpayers have more tax to pay. However, if you buy gilts through the National Savings Stock Register, interest is paid gross (without any tax deducted) but tax is still payable at the savings rate or the higher rate unless you are a non-taxpayer.

Capital gains tax: Capital gains from the sale of gilts are tax free.

INDEX-LINKED GILTS (BRITISH GOVERNMENT STOCK)
Index-linked gilts are those where the interest (coupon) and capital value (nominal) are increased in line with inflation (as measured by the RPI).

Income tax: Tax is deducted from the interest payments at the savings rate of 20%. Non-taxpayers can reclaim the tax. Higher-rate taxpayers have more tax to pay. However, if you buy gilts through the National Savings Stock Register, interest is paid gross (without any tax deducted) but tax is still payable at the savings rate or the higher rate unless you are a non-taxpayer.

Capital gains tax: Capital gains from gilts are tax free.

✪ PERMANENT INTEREST-BEARING SHARES (PIBS)
Permanent interest-bearing shares are loans from you to a building society, for which you are given fixed-interest stocks that have no redemption date and which are traded on the stockmarket. PIBS, like gilts, pay out a fixed interest twice a year, but are infrequently traded and you might find that a buyer is not so easy to come by. There's also a small risk that the loan might not be repaid and/or interest could be suspended, if the society runs into difficulties. Fixed returns are vulnerable to inflation, too. Income from PIBS is consequently a little higher than that on gilts, reflecting the higher risk.

Income tax: Tax is deducted from the interest payments at the savings rate of 20%. Non-taxpayers can reclaim the tax. Higher-rate taxpayers have more tax to pay.

Capital gains tax: Capital gains from PIBS are tax free.

✪ CORPORATE BONDS
Corporate bonds are loans from you to a company, for which you are given interest-bearing stocks that are traded on the stockmarket and Eurobond market. Most corporate bonds pay interest at a fixed rate during their lifetime and are repaid at a set date in the future. A corporate bond's price can rise and fall on the market depending on the fixed rate of interest it offers, so it is possible to buy and sell corporate bonds and make a capital gain. Or you can buy bonds and hold them to redemption, when you will get back the capital value.

Income tax: Tax is deducted from the interest payments at the savings rate of 20%. Non-taxpayers can reclaim the tax. Higher-rate taxpayers have more tax to pay. But, corporate bonds can be held in a PEP with all of the interest tax free (see page 87).

Capital gains tax: Capital gains from qualifying corporate bonds are tax free. But, where bonds are issued at a very low price compared with the amount to be paid back at redemption (deep discount securities), or where the interest offered is very low, any gain you make may be treated as rolled-up income, and will be taxable under income tax, unless the bonds are held in PEPs.

✪ Convertible bonds

Convertible bonds are a type of corporate bond which give you the option of giving up the bond at a set date and receiving ordinary shares in a company. They generally pay less interest than ordinary corporate bonds.

Income tax: As for corporate bonds (see page 79).

Capital gains tax: As for corporate bonds (see page 79).

Local authority bonds

Local authority bonds are loans from you to local government, for which you receive fixed-term, fixed-interest bonds. These bonds must be held to redemption, when you get back your original capital. During the term of the bond you receive fixed interest, usually half-yearly. Bond terms are usually two to eight years.

Income tax: Tax is deducted from the interest payments at the savings rate of 20%. Non-taxpayers can reclaim the tax. Higher-rate taxpayers have more tax to pay.

Capital gains tax: None.

Insurance-based investments

Life insurance: endowment policy – regular premium

Endowment policies are life insurance policies with an investment element. Policies are designed to run for a specified length of time (the endowment period), and pay out a specified assured sum if you die during this time, or, at the end of the time, pay out a cash sum.

Charges are deducted from your contributions, mainly in the early years of the policy, so you generally get a very poor deal if you cash in this type of policy early. Endowments are therefore long-term investments and you need to be locked in for the full policy term – usually a minimum of ten years.

Regular premium endowment policies qualify for special tax treatment. Provided certain conditions are met, you personally pay no tax on the proceeds of the policy. But the investment is taxed (except in the case of Friendly Society tax-free plans) because the insurance company has to pay corporation tax on the returns from investing the money. This is deemed to be equivalent to tax at the savings rate of 20%. Until 1984, premiums qualified for tax relief, but that no longer applies. These policies are not as tax efficient as pure investments, such as unit trusts held in PEPs.

Income tax: Tax equivalent to the savings rate of 20% is deducted from the policy. Non-taxpayers cannot reclaim this tax. Higher-rate taxpayers have extra tax to pay.

Capital gains tax: Capital gains in the form of an endowment policy payout are tax free.

LIFE INSURANCE: ENDOWMENT POLICY– SINGLE PREMIUM

Single premium endowment policies are set up with a single premium rather than regular monthly premiums, but work in the same way as regular premium policies (see above). They also qualify for special tax treatment: you personally pay no tax on the proceeds of the policy, but the investment is taxed because the insurance company pays corporation tax on the underlying investment fund. This is deemed to be equivalent to income tax at the savings rate of 20%. Non-taxpayers cannot reclaim this tax. Higher-rate taxpayers must pay extra tax, but can claim tax relief. Lower-rate and basic-rate taxpayers have no further tax to pay but their age-related tax allowances may be affected: the whole gain on the policy will be added to their income for the year, losing them some or all of the extra tax allowance.

Special rules let you take an income (strictly you are cashing in part of the policy) each year while putting off any higher-rate tax due when the policy finally matures. This income is limited to 1/20 of the premium you paid for a maximum of 20 years. Non-taxpayers should avoid single premium endowment policies as tax paid by the insurer cannot be reclaimed. These policies are not as tax efficient as pure investments, such as unit trusts held in PEPs.

Income tax: Tax equivalent to the savings rate of 20% is deducted from the policy. Non-taxpayers cannot reclaim this tax. Higher-rate taxpayers have extra tax to pay.

Capital gains tax: Capital gains in the form of an endowment policy payout are tax free.

LIFE INSURANCE: FLEXIBLE WHOLE-OF-LIFE POLICY

Whole-of-life insurance policies provide life insurance and a unit-linked investment fund where you choose the balance between the insurance and investment elements. They also qualify for special tax treatment: you personally pay no tax on the proceeds of the policy, but the investment is taxed because the insurance company pays corporation tax on the underlying investment fund. This is deemed to be equivalent to income tax at the savings rate of 20%. Non-taxpayers cannot reclaim this tax. Higher-rate taxpayers must pay extra tax, but can claim tax relief. These policies are not as tax efficient as pure investments, such as unit trusts held in PEPs.

Income tax: Tax equivalent to the savings rate of 20% is deducted from the policy. Non-taxpayers cannot reclaim this tax. Higher-rate taxpayers have extra tax to pay.

Capital gains tax: Capital gains in the form of a whole-of-life policy payout are tax free.

LIFE INSURANCE: SINGLE PREMIUM INVESTMENT BONDS

Single premium investment bonds are a form of whole-of-life insurance which give minimal life cover and are used for investment growth. Your single lump sum premium is invested by the insurer on a unit-linked basis. You choose which funds (there may be as many as 20 to choose from) to invest in and can switch between them at any time. You can cash in the bond at any time to take your profits. Investment returns from these bonds are treated as income rather than capital gains, but you personally pay no tax on the proceeds of the policy; the investment is taxed because the insurance company pays corporation tax on the underlying investment fund. This is deemed to be equivalent to income tax at the savings rate of 20%. Non-taxpayers cannot reclaim this tax. Higher-rate taxpayers must pay extra tax, but can claim tax relief. Lower-rate and basic-rate taxpayers have no further tax to pay but their age-related tax allowances may be affected: the whole gain on the policy will be added to their income for the year, losing them some or all of the extra tax allowance.

Special rules let you take an income (strictly you are cashing in part of the policy) each year while putting off any higher-rate tax due when the policy finally matures. This income is limited to 1/20th of the premium you paid for a maximum of 20 years. Non-taxpayers should usually avoid single premium investment bonds as tax paid by the insurer cannot be reclaimed. These policies are not as tax efficient as pure investments, such as unit trusts held in PEPs. However, if you are a higher-rate taxpayer and want to switch funds regularly, or you would have to pay CGT on any capital gains, these bonds may be suitable.

Income tax: Tax equivalent to the savings of 20% is deducted from the policy. Non-taxpayers cannot reclaim this tax. Higher-rate taxpayers have extra tax to pay

Capital gains tax: Capital gains in the form of an endowment policy payout are tax free.

✪ FRIENDLY SOCIETY SAVINGS PLANS OR BONDS

Friendly Society savings plans are a special form of life insurance designed to produce investment growth. They are usually ten-year endowment policies, but unlike most life insurance the return on a Friendly Society plan is completely tax free because the Society is exempt from corporation tax on the underlying investments. The plans can be set up with regular premiums or lump sums. The government restricts the amount you can invest to a relatively low amount: £18 a month or £200 a year in 1997/98. Friendly Society baby bonds are savings plans which can be bought by parents as a gift for children.

Income tax: None – even when bonds are bought by parents as a gift for children (investments bought for children are normally taxed as income of the parent).

Capital gains tax: Capital gains in the form of a Friendly Society savings plan payout are tax free.

INCOME AND GROWTH BONDS

Income and growth bonds offer a fixed income or fixed rate of growth over a set period. With an income bond, your investment can be organised in several ways: one single premium endowment policy from which you take an income; a series of single premium policies with one being cashed in each year; a temporary annuity to provide income together with a deferred annuity to pay back your capital at the end of the period (the deferred annuity is designed with a cash option so you can take a lump sum instead of an income). Similarly, growth bonds can either be based on endowment insurances or on deferred annuities with a cash option. Tax on these bonds depends on the underlying investment used.

Income tax: As endowment policy or annuities.

Capital gains tax: As endowment policy or annuities.

ANNUITIES

Annuities are insurance contracts which provide an income in exchange for a one-off lump sum investment. Income is payable either for life (permanent or lifetime annuity) or for a set period (temporary annuity), and can be level or increasing.

If an annuity has to be bought as part of a pension plan (compulsory purchase pension annuity), the whole of the income is taxed at your highest rate(s) of income tax, and payable under PAYE. If the annuity is bought with a lump sum (purchased annuity), part of the income is treated as return of your original capital and is not taxed. Remaining income is taxed at the savings rate of 20%. If you are a non-taxpayer you can reclaim the tax deducted or arrange for the income to be paid gross (without any tax deducted). Lower- and basic-rate taxpayers have no further tax to pay, but higher-rate taxpayers must pay extra.

Income tax: Income from compulsory purchase pension annuities is taxed at your highest rate(s) of income tax. Income from purchased annuities is partly treated as a return of your capital and is tax free, and the remainder is taxed at the savings rate of 20%. If you are a non-taxpayer you can reclaim the tax deducted or arrange for the income to be paid gross (without any tax deducted). Lower- and

Independent financial adviser and *Moneywise* Ask the Professionals panellist Brian Dennehy says:

"In a nutshell, some life products are tax efficient either because the tax charge within the life company fund may be lower than yours, or because the life product enables you to defer tax until you're paying a lower rate of tax. This is really relevant only for higher-rate taxpayers so if you are a basic-rate or non-taxpayer think carefully whether a life product is relevant to you – for many people there are more tax-effective and cheaper non-life products available."

basic-rate taxpayers have no further tax to pay, but higher-rate taxpayers must pay extra.

Capital gains tax: None.

Stockmarket investments

SHARES

Shares are part ownership of a company which give you the right to have a say in the running of the company by exercising your voting rights at the shareholders' meetings. They also give you the opportunity to share in the profits of the company in the form of dividends.

Shares in public companies are traded on the stockmarket and their prices can rise and fall. Dividend income can vary.

Income tax: Tax is deducted from dividends at a rate of 20%. Non-taxpayers can reclaim this tax. Lower-rate and basic-rate taxpayers have no further tax to pay, but higher-rate taxpayers have extra to pay. However, shares in UK and European Union (EU) companies can be held in PEPs, with dividend income free of income tax. You can hold up to £6,000-worth of shares in a general PEP, and another £3,000-worth of shares in one company in a single company PEP.

Capital gains tax: Capital gains from the sale of shares are taxable at your highest rate of tax. However, you can make total capital gains of up to £6,500 in a tax year with no tax to pay, and shares in UK and EU companies can be held in PEPs, with all gains free of CGT.

SHARES: ALTERNATIVE INVESTMENT MARKET (AIM)

AIM shares are shares in companies quoted on the smaller market of the London Stock Exchange. Typically these are fledgling or expanding companies, raising public money for the first time, but some are well-established businesses often held largely in private hands. Share prices can rise and fall. Dividend income can vary, and may not be paid at all.

Income tax: Tax is deducted from dividends at a rate of 20%. Non-taxpayers can reclaim this tax. Lower-rate and basic-rate taxpayers have no further tax to pay, but higher-rate taxpayers have extra to pay.

Capital gains tax: Capital gains from the sale of shares are taxable at your highest rate of tax, but you can make total capital gains of up to £6,500 this tax year with no tax to pay, and capital losses can be used to reduce CGT bills on other assets either in the same tax year or in future years.

UNIT TRUSTS

Unit trusts are funds of stockmarket investments divided into equal units. Investments are bought by pooling the money of a large number of investors who buy units in the trust. These units have a value that is directly based on the net asset value of the fund's investments, so the value of the units fluctuates according to how well the fund is performing. Unit trusts can pay you out an income based on the income and dividends produced by the investments held in the fund, or the income can be reinvested in more units. Unit trust prices can rise and fall in line with the value of the fund's investments, producing gains or losses.

Income tax: Tax is deducted from unit trust income distributions at a rate of 20%. Non-taxpayers can reclaim this tax. Lower-rate and basic-rate taxpayers have no further tax to pay, but higher-rate taxpayers have extra to pay. When you invest in a unit trust, part of the price may reflect income yet to be paid out. This is refunded when the first distribution is made – an equalisation payment. It is not taxable and is deducted from your initial investment for CGT purposes. However, unit trusts that are 50% invested in UK and EU companies can be held in PEPs, with all income free of income tax. You can hold up to £6,000-worth of qualifying unit trusts or £1,500 worth of non-qualifying (non-UK or non-EU) unit trusts in a general PEP.

Capital gains tax: Capital gains from the sale of units are taxable at your highest rate of tax, but you can make total capital gains of up to £6,500 in a tax year with no tax to pay, and most unit trusts can be held in PEPs, with all gains free of CGT.

INVESTMENT TRUSTS

Investment trusts are UK companies quoted on the Stock Exchange, which invest in the shares of a wide range of other companies. Investment trust companies issue a set number of shares, which are traded on the stockmarket. An investment trust share price may be either higher or lower than the underlying value of the investments it holds because it too is affected by market sentiment, and demand and supply for the shares in the market. These price movements can produce gains or loses. Investment trusts can also provide you with an income in the form of a dividend based on the income produced by the investments held in the trust.

Income tax: Tax is deducted from investment trust dividends at a rate of 20%. Non-taxpayers can reclaim this tax. Lower-rate and basic-rate taxpayers have no further tax to pay, but higher-rate taxpayers have extra to pay. However, investment trusts that are 50% invested in UK and EU companies can be held PEPs, with all income free of income tax. You can hold up to £6,000-worth of qualifying unit trusts or £1,500 of non-qualifying (non-UK or non-EU) unit trusts in a general PEP.

Capital gains tax: Capital gains from the sale of investment trust shares are taxable at your highest rate of tax, but you can make total capital gains of up to £6,500 in a tax year with no tax to pay, and most unit trusts can be held in PEPs, with all gains free of CGT.

INVESTMENT TRUSTS: ZERO-DIVIDEND PREFERENCE SHARES

Zero-dividend preference shares, known as zeros, are investment trust shares with a fixed life of up to ten years, a fixed redemption price, and first call on the total assets of the trust. They do not produce income, only capital growth, but by taking capital gains on a regular basis and using your annual CGT allowances, you can, in effect, produce a tax-free income. Zeros are complex investments, and high risk, so you should take specialist advice.

Income tax: None.

Capital gains tax: Capital gains from zero-dividend preference shares are taxable at your highest rate of tax, but you can make total capital gains of up to £6,500 in a tax year with no tax to pay.

✪ PERSONAL EQUITY PLANS (PEPs)

PEPs are not investments, they are tax-free plans in which you can hold UK shares, shares quoted on a recognised stock exchange in another EU country, certain types of corporate bonds and preference shares, and/or unit trusts and investment trusts (though not all trusts qualify for inclusion in a PEP). You can have one general PEP each tax year in which you invest up to £6,000. You can also have one single company PEP each tax year in which you can invest up to £3,000-worth of the shares of one company. A PEP must be run by an approved PEP management company, which will normally charge for this service. It can be used to provide income, growth, or both, depending on the type of underlying investments you choose. You can cash in part or all of your PEP at any time without losing the tax advantages.

Income tax: Income is tax free

Capital gains tax: Capital gains from the sale of PEP investments are tax free.

Derivatives

Derivatives are contracts that give you the obligation or option to buy or sell an underlying investment at some date in the future. Most common derivatives are futures, index futures and options, and their prices generally track the prices of the underlying investments.

Income tax: None. But, if you deal regularly, you might be treated as running a business and have to pay income tax on your profits.

Capital gains tax: Capital gains from the sale or exercise of derivatives are taxed at your highest rate of tax. However, profits on derivatives linked to British government stocks or corporate bonds will usually be tax free.

Futures

Futures are contracts which give you the obligation to buy or sell an underlying investment at some date in the future.

Income tax: None.

Capital gains tax: Capital gains from the sale or exercise of futures are taxed at your highest rate of tax.

Options

Options are a form of derivative giving you the right, but not the obligation, to buy or sell the underlying investment (shares, gilts, etc.) at a set price before a set date.

Income tax: None. But, if you deal regularly you might be treated as running a business and have to pay income tax on your profits.

Capital gains tax: Capital gains from the sale or exercise of derivatives are taxed at your highest rate of tax. However, profits on derivatives linked to British government stocks or corporate bonds will usually be tax free.

Other investments

✪ ENTERPRISE INVESTMENT SCHEMES (EISs)
Enterprise Investment Schemes are schemes giving you tax breaks to invest in the newly issued unquoted shares of UK trading companies. Companies floating on the AIM can be eligible for EIS investment. You must hold the shares for at least five years in order to retain the tax breaks.

Income tax: Income tax relief at the lower rate of 20% is given on the amount you invest up to a maximum of £100,000 a year. For this purpose, investments made up to 6 October can be carried back and treated as if made in the previous tax year.

Capital gains tax: Capital gains from the sale of the shares are free of CGT. Capital losses can be offset against gains on other assets for CGT purposes. EIS investments also qualify for tax if you reinvest proceeds in another scheme.

✪ VENTURE CAPITAL TRUSTS (VCTs)
Venture Capital Trusts are schemes which give you tax breaks to invest in funds of unquoted UK companies, but with less risk than investing through the EIS (see above). VCTs work like a specialist investment trust; you buy newly issued shares in the VCT, which must invest at least 70% of the money raised in unquoted UK trading companies, giving you a stake in a spread of such companies. VCTs themselves are quoted on the stockmarket, hopefully making it possible for you to sell when you want to. You must hold the VCT shares for at least five years to qualify for the tax incentives.

Income tax: Income tax relief at the lower rate of 20% is given on the amount you invest up to a maximum of £100,000 a year. Dividends from the VCT shares are free of income tax.

Capital gains tax: Capital gains from the sale of VCT holdings are free of CGT. VCTs pay no tax on capital gains on the underlying shares, and investments also qualify for reinvestment relief.

PROPERTY, ANTIQUES AND OTHER ASSETS
Antiques, paintings, sculpture, stamps, coins, gold and diamonds are treated as investments for tax purposes when you sell them. They produce no income – in fact, they can cost you money for

storage, security, and insurance. Return depends on market conditions and, if prices fall, you stand to make a loss. You can't be sure of getting your money back quickly, because it might be impossible to find an immediate buyer. Alternatively, a quick sale might mean accepting a lower price and possible loss.

Income tax: None. However, if you buy and sell regularly the Inland Revenue may decide that you are a trader and tax you as if you are getting profits from a business.

Capital gains tax: Capital gains from the sale of property (except your main private residence), antiques and other assets are taxable at your highest rate of tax. However, you can make total capital gains of up to £6,500 in a tax year with no tax to pay.

How to save more on tax investments

YOU CAN SAVE MORE TAX by making full use of the tax allowances available to you – and the tax allowances of other members of your family.

MARRIED COUPLE'S ALLOWANCE

If you are married you should make sure you claim the married couple's allowance. This gives tax relief at 15% on £1,830 for 1997/98 – a maximum saving of £274.50. You have to claim for it on your tax return, or by making a request to your tax office – don't assume your employer will do this for you.

In order to claim you should use Inland Revenue form 11PA. Once you have done so you will receive the allowance automatically each year, either through the PAYE system if you are an employee, or via your accountant, if you're self-employed. It usually goes to the husband, but if the sole wage-earner is the wife you should allocate the allowance to her, using Inland Revenue form 18. You have to make your claim before the start of the tax year for which you want this to apply.

You can also split assets between yourself and your spouse to make full use of both your tax allowances. There are a number areas in which you can do this.

Personal allowances

If you are married and one of you is a non-earner, you can transfer income-producing investments, such as savings accounts and unit trusts, into the non-earner's name. This will allow the non-earner to offset the investment income against the personal allowance – £4,045 in 1997/98. Investment income of up to that amount will then be tax free.

CGT allowances

If you are married and one of you has investments that will produce a large capital when they are sold, you can put the investment into your joint names. This will give you double the annual CGT allowances – £6,500 each person in 1997/98. Capital gains of £13,000 (2 x £6,500) can then be made tax free.

CGT bed-and-breakfasting

You can also spread your overall capital gains across a number of years, and a number of tax allowances, by selling some of your investments each year. This is known as 'bed-and-breakfasting', and it is mainly used to reduce CGT on stockmarket investments. It works like this:

1. You sell stockmarket investments that have produced gains up to a value of £6,500.
2. You pay no CGT tax on them as the gains are covered by your £6,500 annual CGT exemption.
3. You then buy back the same investments the next day, and because you've just bought them, the gain you've made on them is now zero.
4. You repeat the process in the next tax year to soak up another £6,500 worth of tax-free gains.

In this way, you are constantly winding the CGT clock back to zero. You are not letting taxable gains build up in your investments. But bear in mind that you will have to pay commission and charges on the sale and re-buying, so whether or not it is worth doing will depend on the actual amounts involved.

Income tax relief on pension life insurance

If you have a partner or children, you have probably taken out some life insurance. But you can save tax on the cost of the premiums by taking out cover through a personal pension plan, if you have one. You can spend up to 5% of your net relevant earnings on premiums, on which you'll get income tax relief at your highest rate. With a personal pension plan there is no restriction on the amount insured, though this is limited to four times your salary if you have a free-standing additional voluntary contribution (FSAVC) plan.

Offshore investments

OFFSHORE INVESTMENTS ARE any investments held in banks, building societies and fund management companies based outside the UK. And as they are outside the UK tax regime, they pay returns free of all UK taxes. Interest is paid gross. Gains made offshore are not taxable.

But you do still have to declare your offshore investment returns in the UK – and they do become taxable if you receive them in the UK. Even so, this still provides opportunities to reduce or avoid tax. For example, if you are a higher-rate taxpayer and have investments offshore, you can wait to receive your income and gains until you become a lower-rate or non-taxpayer – perhaps when you retire.

These are the main ways in which you can use your offshore investments to save tax:

- Put money into an account with an offshore bank or building society to accumulate interest with no tax deducted – this gives you compound tax-free interest. If you put the money in a UK savings account you would only receive tax-free interest if your total taxable income was below your tax allowances and you completed tax form R85.
- Defer the tax you have to pay on your savings by having the gross interest on an offshore account capitalised as at 1 May – this becomes the date at which your account is taxed but you don't have to declare the gross interest on your account until the following April, or pay your tax bill until several months later.
- Defer the tax you have to pay on savings until you retire, or until you become a lower-rate taxpayer, by keeping your

savings in an offshore account or investment until that time – you could use an offshore roll-up fund that pays no dividend income but provides a return as growth only.

And there are three main types of offshore investment that you can use:

- Offshore savings accounts are offered by subsidiaries of UK high street banks and building societies and work just like UK savings accounts – except that interest is paid without tax being deducted.
- Multi-currency cheque accounts allow you to hold money offshore tax free and write cheques or make payments in more than one currency – this can be useful if you work or own property abroad and need to be able to make payments there and in the UK.
- Offshore investment funds are similar to UK unit trusts or investment trusts – they spread your money across a range of stockmarket investments but with no tax deducted from the returns.

All these offshore investments can be useful if you stand to benefit from deferring tax, or if you have already made full use of all the other UK tax-free savings. Remember, however, regulation in the different offshore investment centres varies. It is therefore advisable to consult an accountant or an independent adviser before making a decision.

Action plan

- Check whether your current savings and investments are tax efficient – if they're not, ask yourself why you have got them. If the reason you took them out no longer applies, consider switching to something more appropriate.
- If you initially made certain types of investment on the basis of tax efficiency, check that this still applies.
- Whenever you are considering making an investment, check out the tax rules first to make sure you understand them and are happy with how you'll be taxed.

TAX

7 Pensions

Tax on pensions is lower than the tax on almost any other form of saving or investment. Tax breaks on pensions can even reduce the total amount of income tax you pay. So it's not surprising that pensions are among the most tax-efficient investments you can make – nor is it coincidental.

Tax rules have been adapted by successive governments to make pension investment attractive, and to encourage you to provide for yourself in retirement.

State pensions are not affected by these tax rules as they are funded by National Insurance and paid with no tax deducted. It is employers pensions and personal pensions that really benefit. There are three ways in which the tax rules work in your favour:

- Tax relief is given on the money you pay into an approved personal or company pension.
- Tax-free capital gains are allowed on the money invested in a pension scheme.
- Tax-free cash can be taken as a lump sum when you retire.

Tax is only payable on the income from pensions, so, in effect, pensions work in the opposite way to tax-efficient investments such as PEPs. Pension money is tax free on the way in, taxable on the way out; PEP money is taxable on the way in, and tax free on the way out. But the combined effect of all the pension tax breaks makes pensions more efficient for long-term savings.

Of course, these tax breaks, taken together, cost the government millions of pounds, so there are there limits on how far you're allowed to benefit from them. The Inland Revenue, which administers the tax rules on pensions, sets an upper limit on the size of pension you can build up, by setting a maximum pension level for employers pension schemes, and by limiting the contributions which can be made to personal pensions. Future governments may have to limit these tax breaks further, and in 1997 Chancellor Gordon Brown showed that the new Labour government is prepared to scrap some of them altogether. In his July Budget he abolished the corporation tax credits which boosted pension funds.

But for income taxpayers like yourself, all the major pension tax breaks are still available, and it's worth taking advantage of them while you still can. Some of the pension tax rules can be complicated, though, so in this chapter, we explain the basic principles of the pension tax rules, and then look at how they affect your state pension, your employers pension and/or your personal pension.

Tax relief on contributions

YOUR CONTRIBUTIONS TO any Inland Revenue approved pension scheme are granted tax relief at your 'marginal' rate of tax. What this means is that any money you pay into a normal employers pension scheme or a personal pension has no tax deducted from it; it is paid direct from your salary, before your salary is taxed.

A £100 pension contribution therefore costs you £100 of pre-tax salary. The Inland Revenue lets you off the tax at your marginal rate. In effect it is giving the tax back to you, to put into your pension. So if you're a basic-rate taxpayer you only give up £77 of taxed salary to pay a £100 contribution – the Inland Revenue gives you the other £23 in basic-rate tax. And if you are a higher-rate taxpayer you only give up £60 of taxed salary for a £100 contribution – the Inland Revenue gives you the extra £40 in higher-rate tax.

It's this tax relief that makes pensions such a cost-effective way to save for retirement. Other investments, even tax-free investments, can only be made using income that has already been taxed, so a £100 investment in a PEP actually costs you £129.87 of your pre-tax salary if you are a basic-rate taxpayer because the Inland Revenue takes 23% of it – £29.87 – before you can invest it. It is even possible that a £100 investment could cost you £166.66 of pre-tax salary if you're a higher-rate taxpayer, because 40%– £66.66 – is taken in tax before you can invest it.

But because pension contributions come out of your tax-free salary, you actually end up paying less income tax. This is because once you've made your pension contributions, the taxable part of your salary is lower. You can see why this happens in the example below.

Example

You are single and have a gross salary of £32,000, but don't yet pay into a pension. Your tax liability is as follows:

	Tax due
Personal allowance of £4,045	£0
First £4,100 of taxable income taxed at 20%	£820.00
Next £22,000 of taxable income taxed at 23%	£5,060.00
Remaining taxable income of £1,855 taxed at 40%	£742.00
Total tax bill	**£6,622.00**

You now start paying into a pension, and make a contribution of £4,000 in the tax year. This is how it reduces your tax liability:

	Tax due
Personal allowance of £4,045	£0
Pension contribution of £4,000 full tax relief	£0
First £4,100 of taxable income taxed at 20%	£820.00
Next £19,855 of taxable income taxed at 23%	£4,566.65
Total tax bill	**£5,386.65**
Difference in tax liability	**£1,235.35**

Tax on pension investments

EMPLOYERS PENSIONS and personal pensions take your contributions and put them into funds of investments, such as shares, cash deposits, and other assets. All these investments are taxable if you hold them directly, but in a pension fund, the investments grow completely tax free.

There is no income tax on the income that these investments produce, and there is no capital gains tax (CGT) on the capital growth – the rise in value – that the pension investments achieve.

It's this tax-free growth that gives pensions the potential to grow faster than any similar investments, and produce a large enough lump sum to provide a retirement income.

Employers pensions and personal pensions used to be free from corporation tax, which meant they could reclaim the tax that was deducted automatically from share dividends they received, and because many pension funds did hold shares – to produce income and growth – this was a valuable tax break. Reclaimed tax was paid to them on a regular basis and was called an advance corporation tax (ACT) credit. But in the July 1997 Budget ACT credits were scrapped.

Pension funds will no longer have these tax credits to boost their investment growth, and as many funds still rely on share investments for growth, pensions will be reduced. Some

> Independent financial adviser and *Moneywise* Ask the Professionals panellist Brian Dennehy says:
>
> "If your pension fund relies heavily on dividends paid out by underlying investments for its year to year growth, the new rules will certainly have a long-term impact on the size of your pension fund. Sensible analysts suggest a growth rate of 9% will fall to 8·25%, which means that someone with 20 years to retirement would need to increase their monthly contributions by about 8%. The precise impact will vary considerably from one pension fund to another, so it is vital to talk this through with your independent financial adviser as a switch of funds may be adequate to deal with the problem."

pension providers estimate that final pension funds will be 10% to 15% lower than they would have been with the ACT credits. How this will affect your employers pension or personal pension is not yet clear – it will depend on how your pension provider makes up for the loss of the tax break. Contact your pension provider or financial adviser to find out how the tax change could affect you.

Tax on pension income

PENSION INCOME that is paid to you is liable to income tax, just like all the income you've received throughout your life. There are no tax breaks or tax reliefs to allow you to take your pension tax free, but you can use your personal tax allowance to reduce the amount of tax you pay.

Your personal allowance is the amount of income on which you do not have to pay any tax at all. There are also additional allowances that can be used to reduce tax on pensions – for married couples and people over retirement age. These allowances are usually increased by the government in line with inflation, and may be adjusted by the Inland Revenue from time to time, to make up for previous over- or underpayment of tax.

For the tax year 1997/98 allowances are as follows:

PERSONAL ALLOWANCES:	£
aged under 65	4,045
aged 65–74	5,220
aged 75 and older	5,400
MARRIED COUPLE'S ALLOWANCES:	
aged under 65	1,830
aged 65–74	3,185
aged 75 and older	3,225

So if you're under 65 you can have income of £4,045 before you pay any tax. A married couple under 65 is entitled to the extra allowance of £1,830, but the tax relief is only at 15%, regardless of whether the taxpayer is a basic- or higher-rate taxpayer. Higher allowances for people over 65 are available subject to an income limit of £15,600 in 1997/98 – for every £2 of income you receive over this limit, your age-related allowance is reduced by £1. Your allowance will not be reduced further than the basic single person's allowance of £4,045.

Income tax due on your pension depends on your total income and your total allowances in a tax year. To work this out, your pension income is added to any other income you receive from employment and investments, and your total allowances are added together. Then, if your income is equal to or less than your tax allowance, you do not have to pay income tax on your pension. If your income is higher than your allowances you only pay tax on the amount in excess of the allowance. Tax is charged at the normal rates of income tax. In 1997/98 the rates are:

First £4,100 of taxable income	20%
Next £22,000 of taxable income	23%
Taxable income over £26,100	40%

Your personal allowance is indicated by the tax code which is issued each year by the Inland Revenue, but you check that it's correct. Your code will appear on your payslip and also on form P2(T) 'Notice of Income Tax Code'. The code number is an abbreviation of your personal allowance – it shortens it simply by missing off the last number – so if your allowances total £5,200, your payslip should show your code as 520.

If you think there is something wrong with your tax code, notify your tax office, and make sure you ask for an assessment of tax paid in previous years as well, in case you've been overpaying (or underpaying) your tax for much longer than you realise. For more advice on allowances, see Chapter 4, and for additional information see Chapter 5.

State pensions

STATE PENSIONS are paid to everyone who has made sufficient National Insurance contributions throughout their working lives, but unlike employers pensions and personal pensions, state pensions are not based on investments.

Your National Insurance contributions are not invested in a fund to produce income or capital growth; they are used to pay the pensions of the current generation of state pensioners. This is known as a 'pay-as-you go' scheme, and because there is no investment – only payment – the tax on state pensions is straightforward.

STATE PENSION CONTRIBUTIONS
State pension contributions are provided by National Insurance, which is deducted from your untaxed salary. There is no tax relief, and National Insurance contributions do not affect your total income tax liabilities.

STATE PENSION GROWTH
National Insurance contributions are not invested, so there is no income tax or CGT on the money you pay. Although it goes into the so-called National Insurance Fund, this is just a collection account, not an investment fund.

STATE PENSION INCOME
State pension income is liable to income tax, but it is paid out with no tax deducted. In many cases, there is little or no tax due on it – it all depends on how much other income you have.

If the basic state pension is your only source of income, it will be covered by your personal allowance and no tax will be due. In 1997/98 the basic state pension of £3,179·80 a year was covered by a personal allowance of £4,045.

If you have other income besides the basic state pension, all of your income is added up to calculate how much tax you owe. If your income is higher than your tax allowances, there is tax to pay. Though this tax is not deducted from your state pension, it will, however, be deducted via PAYE from your employers pension or personal pension, and this is why the tax on your other pensions can sometimes seem higher than it should be – it contains an adjustment for other tax liabilities.

Tax on state pensions may be due to change in future if the government pension review that started in 1997 recommends a new type of state pension. Plans under consideration include an investment-based state pension, which would be liable to tax but probably granted tax-free status. Details of the pensions review and its implications for tax are expected in 1999.

Employers pensions

EMPLOYERS PENSIONS are schemes set up by employers for the benefit of their employees. They are also known as company pensions or occupational pensions. And they have one enormous advantage over other pension plans: your employer contributes to them on your behalf.

With most schemes an employer will contribute much more to the pension than the employee does – typically two-thirds of the total contributions, and in a few cases all the contributions.

There are two main types of employers pension:
- *Final salary schemes*: Your pension is worked out as a proportion of your salary on or near retirement. The exact proportion is based on how long you have been a member of the company pension scheme. Most schemes give you 1/60 of your final salary for every year you are a member. So, after 40 years this would produce a pension of 40 x 1/60 = 2/3 of final salary. This is the maximum proportion you are allowed. Some give only 1/80 of final salary for each year. As an employee you pay in a fixed percentage of your earnings – often 5% (except in non-contributory schemes, where the employer pays all the contributions).
- *Money purchase schemes*: These make no firm guarantee about the final pension you will receive, and are not linked to your salary. What you receive when you retire depends upon how much you and your employer have paid in, how the pension fund has performed, and how much annuity income the fund buys you when you retire. Money purchase schemes are

therefore popular with employers, as they are less of a financial commitment, cheaper to run, and less burdened with regulations.

Although the two schemes have different rules, they work in the same way, and they get the same tax breaks – once they are approved by the Inland Revenue. A pension will be approved provided that the pension scheme is set up as a trust, does not exceed the maximum allowable pension benefits set by the Inland Revenue, and does not use certain high-risk and unregulated investments. Almost all employers pension schemes are now approved by the Inland Revenue and benefit from what is known as the 'exempt approved' status. This allows them to give you tax relief on contributions, tax-free growth, and tax-free lump sums.

Employers pension contributions

Tax relief is given on contributions to employers pension schemes at your highest rate of tax. In most cases the relief is provided by having the contributions deducted from your pre-tax salary under the PAYE system. The Inland Revenue is, in effect, letting you off the tax due on this part of your salary.

You can contribute up to 15% of your salary to an employers pension scheme and AVC scheme (see page 108). Your salary for the purpose of pension contributions is your basic salary plus bonuses, overtime, and other taxable benefits such as company cars, but there is a maximum amount of salary you can base your pension contributions on. This is known as the earnings cap, which is set by the Inland Revenue and usually increased each year. In 1997/98, the earnings cap is £84,000, so the maximum contribution you can make to an employers pension in 1997/98 is £12,600.

Your employer also contributes to your pension, but there is no limit set by the Inland Revenue on how much your employer can contribute.

To work out how much you can afford to pay in, up to the 15% maximum, you can use the contribution calculator overleaf.

If you leave your pension scheme before you have completed two years' membership, you are entitled to a refund of all the contributions you have paid into the scheme. Tax will be deducted from the refund by the Inland Revenue, because your pension contributions were given tax relief when you made them, and the money won't now be used for a pension.

How much can you contribute to your employers pension scheme?

Use this calculator to work out the maximum contributions you can make to your pension:

Annual salary (gross basic on payslip)	£
Annual bonuses, overtime	
Profit-related pay (gross)	
Taxable value (from your P11D) of:	
Company car	
Private health cover	
Mobile phone	
Other benefits	
TOTAL EARNINGS	
Does the Earnings Cap apply? Yes/No	
If Yes and your total earnings are more than £84,000, write £84,000 in Revised Total Earnings below.	
If No, write your total earnings in Revised Total Earnings below.	
REVISED TOTAL EARNINGS	
Maximum pension contribution	
Revised Total Earnings x 15%	

Employers pension growth

Employers pension funds, and the investments they hold, grow free of income tax and CGT, but in 1997, employers pensions lost their exemption from corporation tax – this means that they can no longer reclaim the tax deducted from share dividends. Reclaimed tax used to be paid to them on a regular basis, and was known as an advance corporation tax (ACT) credit. ACT credits were scrapped in the July 1997 Budget, so pension funds will no longer have these tax credits to boost their investment growth.

If you are building up a pension fund that will produce a pension higher than the maximum pension allowed under Inland Revenue rules, steps would have to be taken to reduce the pension. If that was not possible, a pension refund would be paid to you, minus tax.

Employers pension surpluses

When an employers pension scheme builds up a large surplus – it has more money than is needed to pay current and future pensions – the employer can take that money out of the pension fund and put it back into the business. First, though, the employer is expected to use the surplus to make improvements to pensions being paid out to existing pensioners, and also to improve the benefits to current members. Any surplus after that can then be taken by the employer, but the Inland Revenue will tax the surplus because the pension contributions and the investment gains were tax free, and the money is no longer being used for the benefit of pensioners.

Alternatively, if a pension scheme is overfunded the employer can take a 'contributions holiday'. This means that the employer stops making contributions for a specified period, until the surplus in the fund reduces. But employees continue to make contributions. Contribution holidays can only be taken with the agreement of the pension trustees and the pension fund actuary.

Employers pension income

Employers pension schemes can pay you a pension in one of two ways:
- Final salary schemes pay out monthly pension direct to you, usually with tax deducted through the PAYE system. Tax is deducted at your highest rate, and it may seem even higher than that if the tax due on your state pension is also being collected via PAYE.
- Money purchase schemes build up a pension fund which is then used to buy an annuity – an insurance contract that pays you an income for life. Income from the annuity is liable to income tax in the normal way.

You can offset the income from both types of employers pensions against your tax allowances, and your personal tax allowances increase once you are over 65, and again once you reach 75. But remember that there is an earnings limit that reduces the value of the allowances. In 1997/98 the earnings limit is £15,600, and any income over that limit will reduce your age-related personal allowances by £1 for every £2 of income over the limit. However, your age-related personal allowances cannot be reduced to below the normal personal allowance for people under 65, which is £4,045 in 1997/98.

Any pension income above the value of your tax allowances is then taxed at your highest rate of income tax.

Employers pensions tax-free lump sums

Employers pensions can also pay you a lump sum when you reach the scheme's retirement age, and the Inland Revenue allows you to take this lump sum free of income tax and CGT. However, there is a maximum amount you can take tax free; for employers pension schemes this maximum is 1·5 times your final salary – so if your final salary is £50,000, the maximum lump sum you could take would be £75,000.

You are not automatically entitled to this lump sum. You normally build up your entitlement at a rate of 3/80 of final salary for each year of pensionable service, up to 40 years. Therefore, after 40 years you are entitled to a lump sum of 120/80 – or 1·5 times – final salary. With some employers pension schemes the Inland Revenue will allow the lump sum entitlement to build up faster than the 3/80 rate – whether or not you can take advantage of this accelerated rate depends on your scheme and when you joined it. If you joined a scheme before 1987, you would be able to take the full 1·5 times final salary lump sum after 20 years, on an 'uplifted 80th scale'. The table opposite shows how this works.

If you joined between 1987 and 1989, you build up your entitlement at the normal 3/80 a year rate, but if your scheme builds up a pension at a rate faster than 1/60 of salary for each year, an enhanced lump sum may be allowed. Consult your employers pension scheme administrator if you think you might qualify for an enhanced lump sum.

If you joined after 1989, your maximum lump sum entitlement is the greater of:
○ 1·5 times final salary, or
○ 2·25 times the actual pension you have built up before a lump sum is deducted.

But remember that if you do take a lump sum it comes out of the

Years of pensionable service at normal retirement age	Maximum lump sum as a proportion of final salary
1 to 8	3/80 for each year
9	30/80
10	36/80
11	42/80
12	48/80
13	54/80
14	63/80
15	72/80
16	81/80
17	90/80
18	99/80
19	108/80
20 or more	120/80 = 1·5 times final salary

fund that you have built up to pay for your pension, so the actual pension you receive will be reduced if you decide to take a lump sum.

Lump sums can be higher still, in certain circumstances. For example, if you are medically certified as having a very short life expectancy you can exchange your entire pension for a cash lump sum. Part of the whole lump sum will be treated as if it is the tax free lump sum of 1·5 times your salary; remaining sums will be taxed.

If you do take a lump sum and then use it to buy a 'purchased life' annuity, the income from the annuity will be taxed. However, it is taxed more favourably than normal pension income: part of the income from the purchased life annuity is treated as a return of the lump sum you used to buy the annuity, so this part is free of income tax.

Unapproved employers pension schemes

Unapproved employers pension schemes do not qualify for the tax reliefs available to exempt approved pension schemes, because they are designed to provide benefits for employees who already qualify for the maximum tax-free pension in an approved employers scheme. They have the benefit of being unaffected by the earnings cap for post-1989 pension scheme members, and are allowed to exist alongside approved schemes.

There are two main types of unapproved employers pension scheme:

- *Unfunded unapproved retirement benefit schemes (UURBS)*: Benefits are provided by the employer without a specific pension fund being set up. When a member retires, the employer pays the pension on a 'pay-as-you-go' basis.
- *Funded unapproved retirement benefit schemes (FURBS)*: In this type of scheme the employer makes contributions to a specific pension fund, which is usually set up under trust.

Because unapproved schemes do not enjoy the tax breaks allowed to approved schemes, there will be tax due if you use one:

- Pension income and benefits from UURBS are taxable when you take them.
- Contributions made by an employer to a FURBS are treated as a taxable benefit to you, the employee, so you must pay income tax on them. Any lump sum will be tax free, but the pension income will be treated as other income, and taxed again.

Employers pensions AVCs

Additional voluntary contributions (AVCs) can be made to top up your pension contributions, up to the allowed maximum of 15% of salary. They can be paid into a scheme run by your employer, or into a policy run by an insurance or investment company – called a free-standing AVC (FSAVC) policy.

In most employers pension schemes, employees contribute 5% to 6% of their salary, so you could contribute another 9% to 10% of your salary to an AVC scheme.

Inland Revenue tax reliefs and limits apply to AVCs in the same way as they apply to main employers pension schemes. You can contribute a maximum of 15% of salary to a pension plus an AVC scheme. Contributions within the 15% limit are given tax relief at your highest rate of tax. Tax relief is granted by having the contributions deducted from your pre-tax salary. The maximum pension you receive from a pension plus AVC scheme is two-thirds of your final salary.

If you use your employer's AVC scheme, it is the responsibility of the scheme administrators to ensure that your contributions do not exceed the limit, and that your pension will remain within the maximum of two-thirds final salary. They will limit the amount you contribute to prevent you overfunding your pension.

If you have an FSAVC policy, two checks have to be made:
- An FSAVC provider has to check your estimated gross salary for the year with your employer. This information is combined with the proposed contributions to the FSAVCs to ensure you are not contributing more than you are allowed.
- If you are contributing more than £2,400 a year to the FSAVCs, then the FSAVC provider must check that your total contributions – to both your main employers pension and the FSAVCs – will not take your projected pension over the maximum two-thirds final salary limit; this is known as a 'headroom check'. If your contributions to the FSAVCs are less than £2,400 a year, then the headroom check will only be made upon retirement. If you have overfunded your pension at that point, the surplus will be refunded with tax deducted at a rate of 33% for basic-rate taxpayers and 46% for higher-rate taxpayers

When you retire, the pension from your AVC scheme is added to the pension from the main employers scheme. You can then take all the benefits as a pension income, which will be liable to income tax.

However, tax-free lump sums cannot be taken from AVC schemes that were set up from 1987 onwards. They can only be taken from the main employers pension. Only pre-1987 AVC investors have the option of a tax-free lump sum – again of up to 1·5 times final salary.

Employers pension tax status

Employers pensions must be set up under a trust to qualify for exempt approved tax status. A trust is an arrangement under which property – in this case the assets of the pension scheme – is held by one person or a group of people, the trustees, for the benefit of another group of people. The trustees are not, themselves, able to benefit from the property which has been entrusted to them, with the exception that they can also be members of the pension scheme.

When a pension scheme is set up, a trust deed is drawn up which is legally binding and which outlines the powers of the trustees. These are:

- The power to hold the assets of the scheme, subject to the specific powers outlined in the trust deed or in the scheme rules, and to use those assets in a way that is beneficial to the scheme and its members.
- The power to determine all questions arising from the scheme – the trustees are the final point of reference if there is a query about the way the scheme should work.
- The power to carry out any transaction in connection with the scheme.

Trust status enables the pension scheme members to receive all the tax breaks available under the Inland Revenue rules.

Personal pensions

PERSONAL PENSIONS are offered by insurance and investment companies for those people who cannot, for various reasons, be members of company schemes:

- The self-employed.
- Employees whose employers do not operate a pension scheme.
- Employees who do not want to join their employer's pension scheme – the right to opt out of an employers pension scheme dates from 1988 but it is generally inadvisable to choose a personal pension instead of your employer's scheme.

Personal pensions work in a similar way to money purchase employers pension schemes. Your contributions go into an investment fund, and at retirement you can take up to 25% of the money as a tax-free lump sum, and use the rest to buy an annuity. Personal pensions also offer the same tax efficiency as employers pensions. Payments into a personal pension scheme get full income tax relief and the money in the fund is allowed to build up free of tax. Only the regular income from the pension, after you

have started to draw it, is taxable. But there are two fundamental differences between personal pensions and employers pensions:
- Personal pensions do not get contributions from your employer (except under certain employment arrangements), so you must fund them entirely yourself.
- Personal pensions therefore allow you to pay in more than you can to an employers pension, and build up unlimited pension benefits.

PERSONAL PENSION CONTRIBUTIONS

Tax relief is also given on contributions to personal pensions at your highest rate of tax. Your contributions are set against your relevant earnings for that year, but how you actually obtain this tax relief depends on whether or not you are an employee or self-employed:
- If you are an employee, you make your personal pension contributions from your taxed salary. Basic-rate tax relief is claimed back by the pension provider on your behalf and credited to your pension plan. Higher-rate tax relief must be claimed by you, by notifying your tax office either by letter, or through your tax return. Higher-rate relief is not, however, credited to your personal pension – instead, it is paid back to you by adjusting your personal allowance and tax code by the necessary amount.
- If you are self-employed, you have to make your pension contributions out of your earnings. You then notify the Inland Revenue by means of your tax return, and are given tax relief through your tax assessment.

If you are a non-taxpayer, or pay tax only at the lower 20% rate, your pension contributions are still entitled to tax relief at the basic rate of 23%. The Inland Revenue will not attempt to claw back the difference.

You can contribute to a personal pension only if you have relevant earnings for the tax year in question. Your contributions are limited to a proportion of your relevant earnings, but the proportion increases as you get older. So if you're starting your pension late, you have more opportunity to boost your fund with large contributions in the years you have left before retirement. If you are employed and your employer agrees to contribute to your personal pension, your employer's contributions are added to your own

TAX

PERSONAL PENSION CONTRIBUTION LIMITS	
AGE ON 6 APRIL	**MAXIMUM PERCENTAGE OF NET RELEVANT EARNING**
35 or younger	17.5%
36 to 45	20%
46 to 50	25%
51 to 55	30%
56 to 60	35%
61 to 74	40%

contributions to ensure that they do not exceed the permitted limits.

Contribution limits relate to your age at the start of each tax year on 6 April (see table above).

At 75 you have to take your personal pension, so contributions stop at 74.

Net relevant earnings are those which are liable to tax in the UK. They include:

- Income, including bonuses and taxable benefits, which would be subject to UK tax under Schedule E. If you are an employee, you are liable to Schedule E tax, which is normally paid through the PAYE system. Note that your net relevant earnings are your gross income through employment – the sum on which you pay tax.
- Income from property which is related to your employment.
- Income which can be taxed under Schedule D arising from a business or trade. You must deduct business expenses from this income, as well as any losses or capital allowances for which you are making a claim. For a self-employed person, net relevant earnings are, therefore, basically the profits on which you pay tax.
- Income from certain patent rights which are treated as earned income.

Tax expert and *Moneywise* Ask the Professionals panellist Janet Adam says:

"It is important to remember that you obtain tax relief on contributions to a personal pension scheme only if you have sufficient net relevant earnings in either that year or the previous tax year."

> **EXAMPLE**
> You are a woman of 48 who works for a small business which does not run an employers pension scheme. Instead, your employer contributes to your personal pension. In the 1996/97 tax year, which ended on 5 April 1997, you earned £24,000 from your employer, together with a bonus of £2,000. The bonus is taxable, so your net relevant earnings for the 1996/97 tax year are £26,000. This is well beneath the earnings cap of £82,200 for that year.
>
> You are 48 now, and your birthday was on 20 May, so on 6 April 1996, at the start of the 1996/97 tax year, you were 47. At this age you can pay a maximum personal pension contribution of 25% of your net relevant earnings into your personal pension, so the total you can pay into your personal pension for 1996/97 is 25% of £26,000 – or £6,500. Your employer has agreed to pay £2,000 into your pension for the year. That leaves a maximum contribution of £4,500, which you could pay into your pension.

Net relevant earnings do not include pensions, state benefits, or redundancy payments. There are also exclusions which affect company directors. Consult a qualified independent financial adviser if you are in this category.

However, net relevant earnings are subject to the earnings cap limit (£84,000 in 1997/98), so you can only apply the personal pension contributions to a maximum salary of £84,000. Net relevant earnings of more than £84,000 (1997/98) cannot be taken into account when contributing to your personal pension for the 1997/98 tax year.

PERSONAL PENSION EXTRA CONTRIBUTIONS

If you have a personal pension, you can't use AVCs or FSAVCs to make extra contributions. Instead, you can use the carry forward and carry back tax rules to make extra contributions to your pension. These rules allow you to use up any leftover pension contribution allowances from previous tax years.

Carry forward means that if you have not made the maximum contribution allowed in any of the previous six tax years, you can make pension contributions against those allowances. You must use all your current year's allowance first. If you have surplus money to make contributions after that, you must use the oldest years' allowances first. So you can make a far larger contribution to your pension than if you were only able to use your current year's allowance. If you've had a few lean years of trading as a self-employed person, it is a good way of making up for the pension contributions you may have missed. To take advantage of carry forward relief, complete Inland Revenue forms PP42 and PP120. The example on page 114 shows how carry forward works.

Example

You are 38 and have net relevant earnings of £25,000 for the 1997/98 tax year. In addition you have inherited £10,000 which you wish to contribute to your personal pension. This is what you can do:

Tax year	Age	Net relevant earnings	Contribution limit (%)	Maximum allowable contribution	Actual contribution	Unused allowance
97/98	38	£25,000	20%	£5,000	£5,000	£0

You still have £5,000 from your inheritance which you can contribute to your pension. Under carry forward rules you can look at the six previous years, when you had relatively little spare cash, so could not make the maximum allowed contribution in any of them.

Tax year	Age	Net relevant earnings	Contribution limit (%)	Maximum allowable contribution	Actual contribution	Unused allowance
91/92	32	£16,000	17.5%	£2,800	£1,500	£1,300
92/93	33	£17,500	17.5%	£3,062.50	£1,800	£1,262.50
93/94	34	£18,000	17.5%	£3,150	£1,500	£1,650
94/95	35	£20,000	17.5%	£3,500	£2,000	£1,500
95/96	36	£20,000	20%	£4,000	£2,200	£1,800
96/97	37	£22,000	20%	£4,400	£2,500	£1,900

You can therefore contribute the extra £5,000 to your pension using your spare allowances as follows:

Tax year	Available allowance	Contribution
91/92	£1,300.00	£1,300.00
92/93	£1,262.50	£1,262.50
93/94	£1,650.00	£1,650.00
94/95	£1,500.00	£787.50
95/96	£1,800.00	–
96/97	£1,900.00	–

Next year, if you again have money to invest, you still have £712.50 of your 1994/95 allowance to use, as well as £3,700 from your 1995/96 and 1996/97 allowances.

Carry back means you can use up any unused allowance from the previous tax year only, and you can elect to have the contribution treated as if it applies to that tax year. This is useful if you were a higher-rate taxpayer in the previous year, but will not be one in the current year – your pension contribution can be carried back to the previous year when you qualified for tax relief at the higher-rate, or you can delay making a pension contribution in one year – to help your cash flow, for example – and still gain the tax reliefs for that year.

A carry forward payment would also have the same effect, but with carry forward you have to start with the oldest years' unused allowances first, so you can only make a carry forward payment for last year if you have used up all the earlier allowances – and you may not have that much money to contribute. With carry back you can elect to pay a contribution against the previous tax year's allowance without using up any allowances from older years. To take advantage of carry back, complete Inland Revenue forms PP43 and PP120.

It is possible to combine carry forward and carry back when contributing to your personal pension – this way you can benefit from the most recent year first of all, and then direct surplus funds into the older years as well. This is useful if:

○ In your carry back year you had earnings which made you a higher-rate taxpayer, and you were only a basic-rate taxpayer in older years.
○ In your carry back year you have reached an age at which you are entitled to pay a larger proportion of your net relevant earnings into your pension.

In both these cases you will benefit more from the carry back option than the carry forward option, so if you have enough surplus cash, you should elect to carry back first, and then carry forward with any remaining pension contributions.

> **EXAMPLE**
> You have a personal pension to which you have not contributed in the last four years. You now have a cash surplus, and wish to contribute to your pension. Under carry forward you have to start with the unused allowance from four years ago; next, you use up the allowance from three years ago, and so on.
>
> But last year you were a higher-rate taxpayer, and you want to get the maximum tax relief from your contributions. Carry back allows you to make a contribution for last year, regardless of whether or not you have unused allowances in earlier years. Paying your contribution under carry back allows you to use up last year's allowance, and get the higher rate of tax relief.

Personal pension growth

Personal pension funds and the investments they hold also grow free of income tax and CGT, but they also lost their exemption from corporation tax when advance corporation tax (ACT) credits were scrapped in the July 1997 Budget. So personal pension funds will no longer have these repayments of tax to boost their investment growth.

Personal pension income

Personal pensions pay you an income by building up a pension fund which is then used to buy an annuity – an insurance contract that pays you an income for life. Income from the main annuity is liable to income tax in the normal way.

This annuity income is aggregated with any other income you receive, including any pension from the state. You can then offset this income against your tax allowances. Your personal tax allowances increase once you are over 65, and again once you reach 75, but remember that there is an earnings limit that reduces the value of the allowances. In 1997/98, the earnings limit is £15,600. Income over that limit will reduce your age-related personal allowances by £1 for every £2 of income over the limit. However, your age-related personal allowances cannot be reduced to below the normal personal allowance for people under 65, which is £4,045 in 1997/98.

Any pension income above the value of your tax allowances is then taxed at your highest rate of income tax. Tax is normally collected through PAYE operated by the scheme or plan provider, so the correct amount of tax should be deducted automatically.

If your pension looks as if it is being taxed at too high a rate, it may be because PAYE is being used to collect tax on any other income you may have.

Income from an annuity that is bought with a tax-free personal pension lump sum is taxed differently (see below).

Personal pension lump sums

Personal pensions can also pay you a lump sum when you reach the retirement age chosen for your pension, and the Inland Revenue allows you to take the lump sum free of income tax and CGT. However, there is a maximum amount you can take tax free: for all personal pensions, this is 25% of the total pension fund.

> Independent financial adviser and *Moneywise* Ask the Professionals panellist Brian Dennehy says:
>
> "The first calculation in deciding whether to take the lump sum is whether you can generate more income from the tax-free cash than the pension income forgone. The answer is frequently yes, but be careful if the pension income forgone would have been automatically increased each year, perhaps even being index-linked. In the latter situation you need carefully to weigh the valuable flexibility of having the capital against the peace of mind of an indexed pension."

If you then decide to use the tax-free lump sum to buy a 'purchased life' annuity, the income from this annuity will be liable to income tax, but will be taxed more favourably than normal pension income. Part of the income from the purchased life annuity is treated as a return of the lump sum you used to buy the annuity, so this part will be free of income tax. And, since 1996/97, payments from a purchased annuity have been taxed at the lower savings rate of tax – currently 20% – rather the 23% or 40% rates of income tax. If you are a lower- or basic-rate taxpayer there is no further tax to pay. If you are a higher-rate taxpayer there is extra tax to pay which might be collected through PAYE or through a tax assessment. If you are a non-taxpayer you can reclaim the tax or, better still, register to receive the income without any tax deducted; you should arrange this with the insurer providing the annuity.

So an annuity bought with the tax-free lump sum from a personal pension is in fact more tax efficient than the main annuity used to pay the pension income.

If you die before you reach retirement age, your survivors will usually be entitled to the value of the fund accumulated in your pension plan. This is usually paid as a lump sum to your survivors or to your estate; it can also be paid as a pension to the survivors, but the payment of a pension to a dependant must not exceed the pension which would have been payable to you, had you taken retirement the day before your death. In this case, the pension payable to you is considered to be the pension payable if no tax-free cash had been taken – this produces a higher pension, since taking the lump sum reduces the size of the pension.

Personal pension segmented lump sums

You may choose to have your personal pension segmented into a number of separate policies, so that you can take your pension in stages, on different maturity dates. But if you do this, bear in mind that it will affect the amount of tax-free lump sum you can take. You will not be able to take a tax-free lump sum of up to 25% of the whole pension fund – you will only be able to take up to 25% of the segments that have matured. So if you know that you will need the maximum tax-free lump sum on retirement, a segmented personal pension may not be suitable.

Contracted-out personal pensions

Personal pensions may be set up solely for the purpose of contracting out of the state earnings-related pension scheme (SERPS). This is the additional state pension which you qualify for by paying National Insurance. If you contract out of SERPS, this part of your National Insurance contribution is rebated by the Department of Social Security (DSS) and paid into your personal pension. You do not contribute from your earnings, so you do not get tax relief, but basic-rate tax relief is given on that part of the rebate representing a refund of your own National insurance. No higher-rate tax relief is given.

Contracted-out personal pensions invest this money and it grows free of income tax and CGT. When you retire, it pays you a pension which will be equivalent to, or greater than, SERPS, depending on how the investments have performed. Pension income from a contracted out personal pension is taxable. You cannot take a tax-free lump sum from the SERPS-related pension.

Self-invested personal pensions (SIPPs)

SIPPs are personal pensions where you can choose your own investment strategy, or appoint a fund manager to carry the strategy out. Investments can be made in a wide range of shares, property, and assets. They give similar tax breaks to normal personal pensions, but you are not allowed to 'self-invest' or make loans to anyone connected with yourself. Self-investment would be using the pension funds to support your business. You can, however, invest in commercial property, which can then be rented to your business – and the rent will accumulate in your pension fund tax free.

Income from SIPPs is liable to income tax at your highest rate, after you have offset your tax allowances against it. But remember that as SIPPs are specialised pension schemes with complex rules, you should take independent financial advice on the tax implications of setting up a scheme.

Retirement annuity contracts

Retirement annuity contracts were the predecessors of personal pensions, and were set up to allow you to build up a pension fund which you could then use to buy an income-producing annuity. Although no new retirement annuity contracts can be taken out, if you still have one you can continue to contribute to it.

Contributions to retirement annuity contracts are fully entitled to tax relief at your highest rate of tax. If you are an employee or self-employed, you make the contributions gross – without deducting any tax relief. All the tax relief has to be claimed through your tax office. If you are an employee, the relief will usually be given by adjusting your PAYE code; if you are self-employed, relief will be given through your next tax assessment. It can therefore take longer to benefit from the tax relief. There is no earnings cap on Retirement Annuity Contracts. Unlike the regime that applies to personal pensions, if you pay into a Retirement Annuity Contract, you can take all of your income into account – you do not have to disregard that part of your income that exceeds the earnings cap.

Retirement Annuity Contracts are subject to a different set of limits on the amount of net relevant earnings that can be taken into account. The scale is still age related, but the percentages are lower:

Age on 6 April	% of net relevant earnings
aged 50 or under	17.5%
51 to 55	20%
56 to 60	22.5%
61 to 74	25%

Pension fund withdrawal *versus* buying an annuity

On retirement
Personal pension fund: £400,000 (incl. £100,000 lump sum).

Pension fund withdrawal

Defer annuity, and make maximum pension fund withdrawal from fund of £300,000.

Buying an annuity

Buy a single life annuity using fund of £300,000.

Age 60
- £30,900 pension fund withdrawal.
- £30,900 annuity.

Age 63
- £27,534 pension fund withdrawal.
- £30,900 annuity.

Death at age 65. £221,000 pension fund can be inherited by spouse or dependants.

Death at age 65. No further payments.

Age 66
- £24,657 pension fund withdrawal.
- £30,900 annuity.

Age 69
- £22,971 pension fund withdrawal.
- £30,900 annuity.

Age 72
- £20,845 pension fund withdrawal.
- £30,900 annuity.

Age 75 onwards
- £30,900 annuity.
- £30,900 annuity.

Source: Scottish Amicable

It is possible to contribute to both a personal pension and also a Retirement Annuity Contract in the same year, but if you do, the maximum contribution you make – across both plans – will be subject to the limits applying to personal pensions, including the earnings cap.

PERSONAL PENSION DEFERRED ANNUITY PURCHASE

Under the new personal pension rules, it is now possible to defer buying an annuity with the personal pension fund, but still take a tax-free lump sum when you reach your chosen retirement age. This lump sum is limited to a maximum of 25% of the fund. You could take a tax-free lump sum and use it to buy a purchased life annuity while you wait to buy the pension annuity with the rest of your pension fund.

If you die while deferring the buying of the main pension annuity, your spouse or dependant can take your pension fund as a lump sum. Tax is deducted from the sum that is inherited, at a rate of 35% but even with this tax liability, deferred annuity purchase still gives your spouse or dependants the chance to inherit your pension, which they cannot do after you have bought your pension annuity. If your fund is inherited it will count as part of your estate for inheritance tax purposes.

Action plan

- If your employer offers a pension scheme, find out about joining it – there's tax relief on contributions.

- If you're self-employed, or your employer doesn't offer a pension scheme, look into taking out a personal pension – you can make different levels of tax-free contributions according to age.

- If you've been working for a while and decide to take out a personal pension, get professional advice about the carry forward rules to see if it makes sense for you to make up for lost time.

- If you're in an employers scheme and you want to make extra contributions, look into AVCs or FSAVCs.

- If retirement is approaching, work out whether you want to take a tax-free lump sum, and if you're in a personal pension, start shopping around for an annuity.

TAX

8 Capital gains tax

Capital gains tax (CGT) is charged on the profit you make from selling an investment or some other asset for more than you paid for it. You are still treated as having made the profit, even if you dispose of the asset in another way, for example by giving it to someone, or even losing it.

So at its simplest, you deduct the original cost from the proceeds (or market value of the asset you give away) to establish the gain. Under the rules, there are circumstances where CGT doesn't apply, and ways to reduce any gain:

- Some assets are exempt.
- Some transactions are exempt.
- You can deduct various expenses in calculating your profit.
- You can ignore any gain which is simply due to inflation.
- You can often set losses made on one asset against the gains made on another.
- You have an annual allowance which lets you make a certain amount of gains each year totally tax free.
- You may be able to defer paying a CGT bill by claiming reinvestment relief.
- You may be able to pass your CGT bill to the new owner by claiming holdover relief.
- You may be able to reduce or eliminate a CGT bill by claiming retirement relief.

Assets that are exempt
- Sterling currency, including sovereigns minted after 1837.
- Foreign currency for your personal use.
- Personal possessions with a useful life of 50 years or less.
- Your only or main home.
- Private cars and motorbikes.
- Proceeds of life insurance policies, except secondhand policies.
- Proceeds of National Savings investments and Premium Bonds.
- Gains on British government stocks, local authority stocks, and most corporate bonds.

- Gains on shares and other investments held in a PEP (see Chapter 6).
- Shares held through the Enterprise Investment Scheme (EIS) or in a venture capital trust (VCT), provided the tax rules are met.

TRANSACTIONS WHICH ARE EXEMPT
- Gifts between husband and wife.
- Donations to charities and similar organisations.
- Gifts for the public benefit, or land or buildings of outstanding historical interest, for example.
- What you leave when you die.

EXPENSES YOU CAN DEDUCT
You can also deduct from the proceeds any costs that increase the value of the asset (not those for maintenance or repairs) and any directly related to the buying and selling of the asset or investment. These will also be adjusted for inflation (see below).

ALLOWING FOR INFLATION
You are not expected to pay CGT on any increases in the value of assets or investments due solely to inflation. To work out how much this is, calculate the change in the Retail Prices Index (RPI) between the time you bought the asset or incurred a relevant expense and when you dispose of the asset. If this turns your gain into a loss, there is no CGT bill, but you cannot set the loss against other gains (see page 126), and you cannot use it to increase the size of a loss.

To work out the change in the RPI, take the RPI for the month you dispose of the asset or investment and deduct the RPI for the month in which you bought it. Divide this figure by the RPI for the month when you bought the asset – this gives you the indexation factor. Multiply the original cost by the indexation factor, which gives you the indexation allowance that can be used to reduce your gain.

The table on the opposite page gives the RPI statistics for the period 1982 to 1997. You can also get hold of the figures you need in *Moneywise* magazine each month, or from your tax office.

For something you started to own before 31 March 1982, life is a little more complicated. The system of indexation allowances was introduced only from that date and you have to make a

Retail prices index

	Jan	Feb	Mar	Apr	May	Jun	Jul	Aug	Sep	Oct	Nov	Dec
1982	–	–	79.44	81.04	81.62	81.85	81.88	81.90	81.85	82.26	82.66	82.51
1983	82.61	82.97	83.12	84.28	84.64	84.84	85.30	85.68	86.06	86.36	86.67	86.89
1984	86.84	87.20	87.48	88.64	88.97	89.20	89.10	89.94	90.11	90.67	90.95	90.87
1985	91.20	91.94	92.80	94.78	95.21	95.41	95.23	95.49	95.44	95.59	95.92	96.05
1986	96.25	96.60	96.73	97.67	97.85	97.79	97.52	97.82	98.30	98.45	99.29	99.62
1987	100.0	100.4	100.6	101.8	101.9	101.9	101.8	102.1	102.4	102.9	103.4	103.3
1988	103.3	103.7	104.1	105.8	106.2	106.6	106.7	107.9	108.4	109.5	110.0	110.3
1989	111.0	111.8	112.3	114.3	115.0	115.4	115.5	115.8	116.6	117.5	118.5	118.8
1990	119.5	120.2	121.4	125.1	126.2	126.7	126.8	128.1	129.3	130.3	130.0	129.9
1991	130.2	130.9	131.4	133.1	133.5	134.1	133.8	134.1	134.6	135.1	135.6	135.7
1992	135.6	136.3	136.7	138.8	139.3	139.3	138.8	138.9	139.4	139.9	139.7	139.2
1993	137.9	138.8	139.3	140.6	141.1	141.0	140.7	141.3	141.9	141.8	141.6	141.9
1994	141.3	142.1	142.5	144.2	144.7	144.7	144.0	144.7	145.0	145.2	145.3	146.0
1995	146.0	146.9	147.5	149.0	149.6	149.8	149.1	149.9	150.6	149.8	149.8	150.7
1996	150.2	150.9	151.5	152.6	152.9	153.0	152.4	153.1	153.8	153.8	153.9	154.4
1997	154.4	155.0	155.4	156.3	156.9	157.5	157.5	157.5				

CAPITAL GAINS TAX

choice. Either you use the value of the investment on 31 March 1982 as the initial value, using indexation from that date and ignoring any allowable expenses incurred before then; or you use the initial value on the date you actually did first start to own the investment, taking account of all the allowable expenses since then, but taking into account only inflation since 31 March 1982. You should choose whichever method gives you the lower tax bill.

Losses

If you make a loss on one disposal and a gain on another in the same tax year, you can deduct the amount of the loss from the gain. If you make a loss but no gains, you can carry the loss forward and deduct it from any gains made in later years. If you haven't used a loss after six years, you can no longer carry it forward. You should tell the Inland Revenue about the loss in your tax return for the year in which you make the loss. So, if you make a loss in the 1997/98 tax year you must claim the loss by 31 January 2004.

Reliefs

- *Holdover relief*: If you give away business assets, such as shares in your family company, or you make a gift on which inheritance tax is payable, such as a gift into a discretionary trust, you and the recipient can jointly claim holdover relief, which has the effect of transferring your gain to the new owner and deferring any potential tax bill until the new owner disposes of the asset.
- *Reinvestment relief*: If within a period running from one year before you dispose of the asset on which you have made a chargeable gain, up to three years afterwards, you invest in the shares of certain unquoted companies, either direct or through an EIS or VCT, you can claim relief for reinvesting the gain in these shares. The relief defers the tax bill until you eventually sell the shares.
- *Retirement relief*: If you are aged 50 or more and retiring from your business you may be able to claim retirement relief on any gains on the disposal of your business assets.

ANNUAL EXEMPT AMOUNT

You can make a certain amount of capital gain each tax year, tax free. For the 1997/98 tax year the allowance is £6,500. You deduct this once you have worked out any gains and set any losses against them.

HOW MUCH TAX YOU PAY

If you do have CGT to pay, your gain is added to your taxable income for the year, and the gain is then taxed as if it were your top slice of income, so you could pay CGT at the lower, basic or higher rate. If adding the gain to your income takes you over a tax threshold, part of your gain will be taxed at one rate, and part at another.

EXAMPLE

If you sell your second home in February 1997 for £64,000, you will work out whether there's any CGT to pay as follows:

1. Work out what it has cost you. Say you paid £40,000 for it in May 1990 – this is its initial value. If you spent £4,000 on improvements to the house in June 1992 – this is an allowable expense. If you deduct the initial value and the allowable expense from the sale proceeds, you arrive at a gain of £20,000.

2. Next you need to take account of inflation over the period for which you have owned the home. You take the RPI for the month you bought it (126·2 for May 1990), and for February 1997 when you sold it (155·0). The indexation factor is 0·228 (155·0 less 126·2 divided by 126·2). Multiply the initial value by the indexation factor which gives £9,120. You do the same thing for the allowable expense: 155·0 less 138·8 divided by 138·8. Multiply £4,000 by 0·117 to give the indexation allowance of £468. Add them together to give the total indexation allowance of £9,588, which can be deducted from the gain worked out above. This gives a chargeable gain of £10,412.

3. If you have no other chargeable gains in the year, you can now deduct the annual tax-free amount: £6,500 for the 1997/98 tax year. This leaves you with a gain of £3,912 on which you have to pay tax.

4. This will be added to your taxable income to establish how much tax you pay. You pay tax at 40% on any income over £26,100, so if your income is £30,000 the whole of the gain would be liable to CGT at 40%. This would be £1,564·80.

CAPITAL GAINS TAX

INVESTMENTS

These calculations are relatively straightforward if you are looking at a single investment which you have bought and sold, but the position is not quite so easy if you have a whole series of shares in the same company or units in the same trust but bought at different times – how do you decide which shares or units you sold? There are special rules for this. Shares and units are pooled and treated as having been disposed of in the following order:

- Shares or units bought on the same day as the sale (or other disposal).
- Shares or units bought up to ten days before the sale.
- Shares or units acquired on or after 6 April 1982.
- Shares or units acquired between 6 April 1965 and 5 April 1982.
- shares or units acquired before 6 April 1965 (unless you pool these with the 1965/82 shares).

Where shares are lumped together in one of these groups, you match your sale to the most recently acquired shares first and work backwards.

A special concession applies to unit trusts and investment trusts if you are investing through a monthly scheme. Strictly speaking, each monthly payment is a different investment.

To reduce the calculations, you can ask permission to add together all your payments for the trust's accounting year and (after deducting minor withdrawals) have them treated as a single investment made in the seventh month. Distributions which are reinvested are also to be scooped up into this simplified calculation.

If you have shares received as a result of a rights issue or bonus issue, these belong to the same pool as the original shares they were based on. When you sell rights issue shares, you take the cost of the original shares plus the cost of the rights issue shares. Deduct the relevant indexation allowance from each, and add the results together and divide by the total number of shares. Then multiply the result by the number of shares that you sold.

Bonus shares are free, but this will still affect the cost. If you buy 2,000 shares for £4,000, and then receive 500 bonus shares, the cost per share for CGT purposes falls from £2 to £1·60.

Example

You owned shares in the same company acquired as follows:

6 September 1985	2,000 shares @ £1 each	£2,000
4 July 1993	2,000 shares @ £5 each	£10,000
3 May 1996	500 shares @ £6 each	£3,000
	4,500 shares	£15,000

And you sold 1,000 shares on 12 December 1996 @ £6.50 each, and 1,000 shares on 5 February 1997 @ £7.00 each.

You work out the capital gain on the first disposal as follows:
You didn't buy any shares on the day of the sale, or in the previous ten days, so all your shares belong to the pool of those acquired since 1982.
You need to work out the indexation allowance for each set of shares.

Shares acquired 6 September 1985

RPI for December 1996 is 154.4 and the RPI for September 1985 is 95.44, so the indexation factor is 154.4 less 95.44 divided by 95.44, which is 0.618.
Therefore the allowance is 0.618 multiplied by £2,000, which is £1,236.

Shares acquired 4 July 1993

RPI for July 1993 is 140.7, so the indexation factor is 154.4 less 140.7 divided by 140.7, which is 0.097.
Therefore the allowance is 0.097 multiplied by £10,000, which is £970.

Shares acquired 3 May 1996

RPI for May 1996 is 152.9, so the indexation factor is 154.4 less 152.9 divided by 152.9, which is 0.010.
Therefore the allowance is 0.010 multiplied by £3,000, which is £30.

The total indexation allowance is £1,236 plus £970 plus £30, which is £2,236. Add this to the original cost to get the indexed value of the pool: this would be £17,236. Divide this by 4,500 to get the value per share which is £3.83. You sold 1,000 shares, so you can deduct £3,830 from the sale proceeds of £6,500 to get the gain: £2,670.

To work out the gain on the next disposal you can use the indexed value of the remaining pool. This is £17,236 less £3,830, which is £13,406. The RPI for February 1997 is 155.0, and for December 1996 is 154.4, so the indexation factor is 155.0 less 154.4 divided by 154.4, which is 0.004. The allowance is £54. This means the new indexed value of the pool is £13,460. Divide this by 3,500 to get the value per share, which is £3.85. You sold 1,000 shares so you can deduct £3,890 from the sale proceeds of £7,000 to get the gain: £3,150.

Forward planning can help keep a tax bill down. You can reduce the total gain you have on your assets each year by using up the annual allowance. You sell enough of your investments to generate a gain up to the annual exempt amount, then buy them back again the following day. This is called bed-and-breakfasting.

YOUR HOME
The fact that you don't have to pay CGT on any gain made when you sell your home is obviously a bonus. If you have more than one property, you get the exemption on one home only. A married couple can have only one main home, unless they are separated. You can choose which one is your main home for CGT purposes. Remember, you can't choose which one you get MIRAS on or from which you can get a tax-free income under the rent-a-room scheme (see Chapter 4). Your main home for CGT purposes can be different from the one on which you get mortgage interest relief.

Independent financial adviser and *Moneywise* Ask the Professionals panellist Rebekah Kearey says:

"There are two potential pitfalls with bed-and-breakfast activity. The first is the movement of prices. If the value of the asset increases dramatically overnight, you buy it back at a higher price and lose out. Of course, if it drops overnight you gain. The other danger is the cost of sale and repurchase. The potential tax saving must outweigh the charges that could be incurred to sell and repurchase or no saving is made."

If you have a home in a town, and a cottage in the country at which you spend weekends and holidays, your town home will be eligible for MIRAS, but your main home for CGT could be either property. You should obviously choose as your main home for CGT the one on which you are likely to make the largest gain when you sell it.

Once you have acquired a second home you have two years in which to notify your tax office of which is the main one for CGT. You can backdate your decision by up to two years, and can change your mind and again backdate your decision by two years.

If you have two homes – one you own, the other you rent (or it goes with your job) – don't assume that the one you own will be your main home for CGT purposes – make sure you nominate the one you own as your main home. If you don't nominate one of the homes, your tax office will make the decision based on the facts, in other words the home which really is your main home.

> Independent mortgage adviser and *Moneywise* Ask the Professionals panellist Walter Avrili says:
>
> "Increases in the value of your main residence are currently exempt from CGT. With house prices historically increasing at more than the rate of inflation, and with property representing most families' major asset, this exemption is a huge bonus for most UK households. And, not having to pay CGT on a house sale generally helps the flow of property transactions. Many people would be loathe to sell and move upmarket if faced with a significant tax bill."

There are certain circumstances in which you don't have to live in the home you have chosen as your main home for CGT:

- Absence in the early years – if you can't move into your new home because it is being built, redecorated, or having works carried out on it, or because you can't sell your old home. You won't lose the exemption for the first year (or two years if there's a good reason) provided you eventually live in it during the first year (or two years).
- Absence in the last years – the last three years before you give away or sell the home are exempt, even if you have nominated another home as your main home for CGT.
- Absence at anytime – you can be away for a period totalling three years without any specific reason.
- Absence because of your job – if you were working outside the UK, the period of that employment is exempt. You can claim the exemption for up to four years if you have to live away from your home because of your job.

Action plan

- If you've sold or given away any investments, valuables, or property this year, check whether they're on the list of items exempt from CGT.

- If you have sold or given away any investments which are not exempt from CGT, and you made gains of more than £6,500, follow our instructions to work out the tax bill.

- If you own shares in a company which you bought at different times and you sell some, there are special rules for working out the taxable gain.

- If you have more than one home, choose the one on which you'd make the larger gain as your main home for CGT purposes – or the one you think you're likely to sell soonest.

TAX

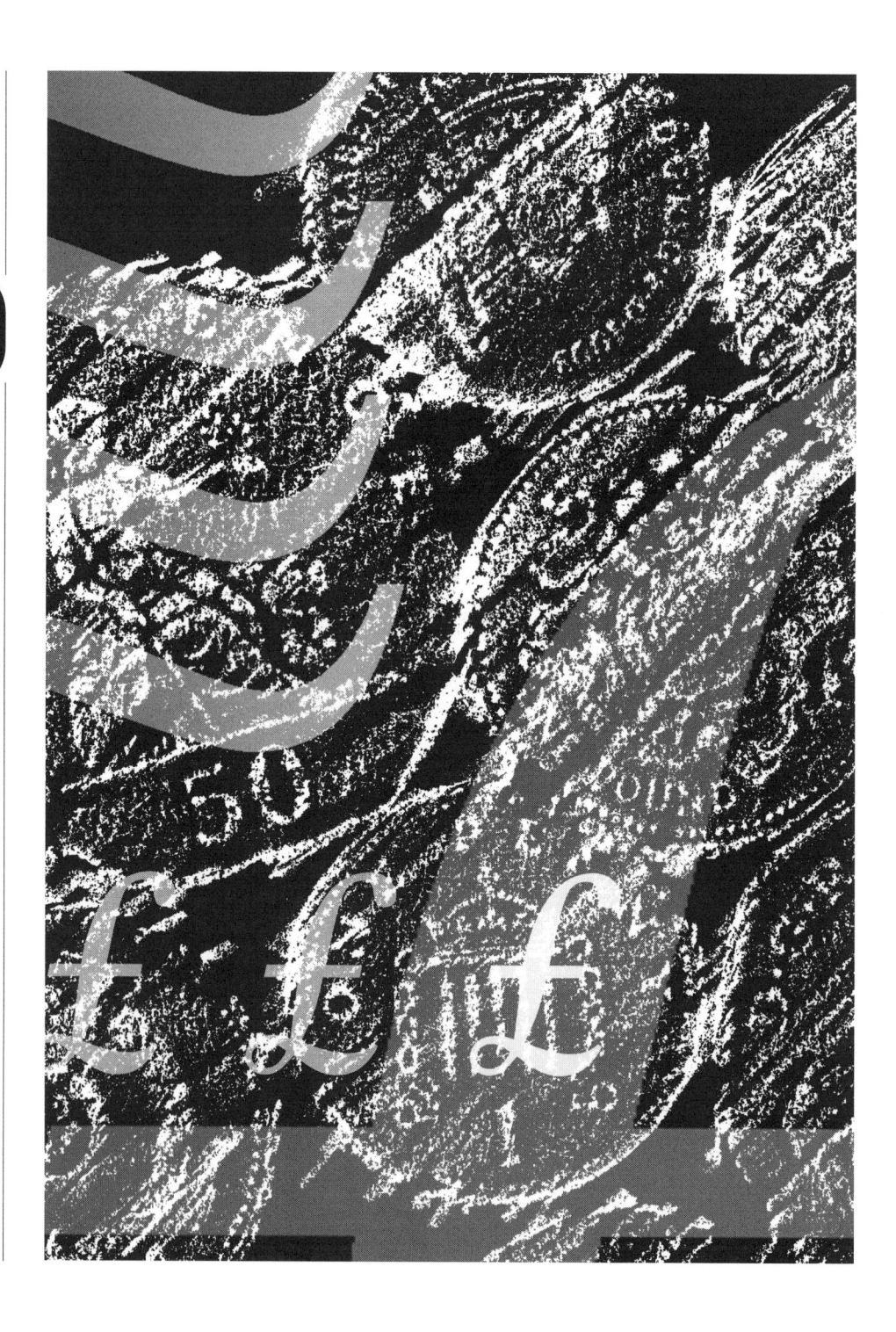

9 Inheritance tax

There may be tax to pay when you die, depending on what you leave behind. This tax is still sometimes cheerfully called death duty, but its official name is inheritance tax (IHT).

Whether any tax is due depends on the size of your estate. This includes:
- Anything owned in your name.
- Your share of anything owned jointly with others.
- Anything held in trust from which you benefit.
- Anything you've given away, but kept some benefit from, for example, a house you live in and used to own.

IHT doesn't just arise on death – it can be payable on gifts you make during your lifetime. But we'll start with the gifts and bequests you won't have to pay tax on:
- Each parent can give up to £5,000 to a son or daughter as a wedding gift, each grandparent can give £2,500, and others can give £1,000.
- Any number of gifts of up to £250 a person a year are tax free.
- Gifts which count as coming from your normal expenditure are tax free.
- You can make gifts up to £3,000 each year tax free. If this allowance is not used up one year, the unused part can be carried forward to the next year (but not to any subsequent year). This means you could make up to £6,000 of gifts tax free in one year.
- There is no IHT on a gift at the time it is made, and none at all provided you survive for seven years after making the gift. These gifts are called 'potentially exempt transfers'. If the £3,000 allowance described above hasn't been used up, the annual allowance will be set against potentially exempt gifts if they do become taxable.
- When you make a gift which counts for IHT or on death all your chargeable gifts over the seven years up to the date of the latest gift or death are added together, tax is payable only if this total comes to more than the 'nil rate band' (£215,000 in 1997/98).

○ Anything left to your spouse is tax free.
○ Gifts to UK charities, gifts to a political party (usually those represented in the House of Commons) and gifts to a national museum can be made tax free.

To work out whether there is any tax to pay, you take the following steps:

1. Identify everything in the estate.
2. Exclude anything that is exempt.
3. Add in any gifts made in the seven years prior to death and any gifts on which the deceased had retained an interest.
4. Value everything that forms part of the taxable estate.
5. Deduct the nil rate band (£215,000 in 1997/98).

If as a result of these calculations IHT is due, it is payable at different rates on the estate and on gifts made in the previous seven years. On the estate it is levied at a single rate which, for 1997/98, is 40%. Tax due at death on gifts made in the seven years before death is on a sliding scale:

Up to 3 years	40%
Between 3 and 4 years	32%
Between 4 and 5 years	24%
Between 5 and 6 years	16%
Between 6 and 7 years	8%

For IHT purposes, gifts are valued as the loss to the giver, rather than the benefit to the recipient.

Sometimes there will be IHT due on gifts made before death, such as gifts to discretionary trusts and to certain companies. But IHT is due only when the total figure for all your gifts over the seven years up to the time of death comes to more than the nil rate band. Tax on anything over this amount is half the rate on death, so it is 20% in the tax year 1997/98. If you die within seven years of making the gift, the tax is re-assessed at the rates which apply on death (see the table above).

Cutting your IHT bill

YOU DON'T HAVE to leave any IHT bill to chance. It is worth working out what your liability might be if you were to die today to get an idea of what tax there might be to pay.

Independent financial adviser and *Moneywise* Ask the Professionals panellist Rebekah Kearey says:

"It is never too early to start inheritance tax planning. The current threshold may seem high now, but future legislation may alter the situation. It is surprising how quickly assets start to build in value once you include things like property. Early planning often allows you to use the cheapest options and to maintain greater flexibility."

There are ways to reduce the IHT bill for your heirs, but you need to decide whether it's worth the effort first, for example, if you know your taxable estate will be worth £235,000, that's £20,000 over the nil rate band. Tax on that at 40% is £8,000.

Nobody would turn their nose up at £8,000, but even after tax there would be £227,000, so in this case it's probably not worth getting involved with any complex tax arrangements. You could consider making small gifts as time goes by, but this may not be easy to do if your estate is tied up in your home or other assets you use. You may be able to organise some of the basic steps to cut a bill yourself, but it makes sense to consult a professional if there are more complex arrangements to make.

If your heirs could face a high IHT bill, it makes sense to plan ahead to minimise the bill. To make sure you get it right it's best to consult a solicitor, accountant or tax consultant. If you're married and have children you could make sure your will incorporates leaving some of your estate to your children; that way you and your spouse will be able to use the nil rate band.

There are two main ways to reduce an IHT bill: you can redistribute your assets or shelter them. A combination of both strategies may be the answer in many cases.

Redistribution entails giving your money and assets away to reduce your worth before you die. It clearly needs careful thought as you don't want to leave yourself with undue financial constraints or in difficulty – you'll need to bear in mind costs you might incur for care later in life before handing out your savings.

If you're married, it is a good idea to redistribute your wealth so that both your estates would be equal. If one spouse has the substantial share of a couple's wealth, the options for keeping the IHT bill down could be limited. Sharing wealth out means that each person can make use of the annual £3,000 exemption, the opportunity to make tax-free small gifts, and their nil rate band. And as each spouse has wealth of his or her own, each of them can leave part of their estate to children or grandchildren. Without this redistribution, there might be no IHT bill when the first spouse dies, but a large amount to pay on the second death.

If you have a life insurance policy, consider getting it written in trust to your chosen beneficiaries, so that anything paid out won't form part of your estate and so will fall outside the tax net.

> **EXAMPLE**
> Your estate is worth £300,000 and your spouse's estate is worth £100,000. If you leave everything to your spouse, there will be IHT to pay when your spouse dies. This will be 40% of £400,000 less £215,000 (£185,000), which is £74,000.
>
> If on the other hand you leave £215,000 to your children and the balance of £85,000 to your spouse, there'll be no IHT to pay when your spouse dies. Your spouse's estate would be £185,000, which is below the nil rate band.

Your home may be one of your biggest assets and could push you over the IHT threshold, but giving it away to avoid tax is not necessarily the answer. If you own your home jointly with your husband or wife, you may hold it as 'joint tenants' or as 'tenants in common'. A property held as joint tenancy automatically goes to the surviving joint tenant when someone dies. If you are tenants in common, you can choose who inherits your share through your will. You can alter the type of tenancy you have – you'd need to take professional advice.

The advantage of being tenants in common is that one partner can give his or her share away on death – to a son or daughter, for example. Depending on the value of your home, this would be a gift which falls within the nil rate band, and everything else could be left to your spouse and would not be liable to IHT. It could go wrong though if your son or daughter dies first, or if they need to sell the property.

You might think it's worth giving your whole home away, but if you continue to live in the home it will probably be considered a 'gift with reservation' and will still count as part of your estate for IHT purposes. If you pay rent, it might be considered an outright gift, but will the rent you pay, the income tax the new owner has to pay on the rent, and the capital gains tax when the prop-erty is sold outweigh the IHT saved?

If you can afford to, and intend to, make substantial gifts – more than the nil rate band – make them as soon as you can. If you live for three years after making these gifts the tax is reduced on a sliding scale.

Sheltering your assets involves using trusts. You may be reluctant to lose control of your assets, which is essentially what setting up a trust involves, but it can be a very useful step if you're concerned about IHT. For example, you can freeze the value of some of your estate and arrange for any increase in value, which would otherwise have pushed the value of your estate and any IHT bill higher, to go to someone else. This can easily be done using a trust. Any growth in investments put in trust is not counted as part of your estate.

A trust is a legal arrangement. You make your gift to the trustees who hold and manage the assets on behalf of the people you want to benefit – the beneficiaries. The names of the people involved, the details of the type of trust, and the powers the trustees will have are recorded in a trust deed.

You might want to use the following types of trust:

- *Absolute trust*: A trust in which the main details are laid down at the outset and cannot be changed.
- *Accumulation and maintenance trust*: A type of discretionary trust (see below). The trust accumulates income and the trustees are allowed to use it for the education, maintenance or other benefit of any of the beneficiaries. These trusts are often used for children, grandchildren, or other people whom you wish to benefit.
- *Bare trust*: A simple type of trust in which the trustee holds the assets only nominally and is known as the 'nominee'.
- *Discretionary trust*: A form of trust in which the trustees have wide powers to retain or pay out trust income for any one or more of the beneficiaries named.

- *Flexible trust*: A trust in which the trustees can vary the proportion of assets due to the different beneficiaries – the opposite of an absolute trust.
- *Interest in possession/life interest trust*: A trust which entitles the beneficiary to income from the trust for life, though the income-producing assets ultimately pass to a different set of beneficiaries.
- *Loan trusts*: The investor makes a loan to the trustees, who put the money in an insurance bond. The loan is repaid out of regular annual withdrawals from the bond, and the repayments go back into the settlor's estate, but any growth which has accrued to the bond falls outside the estate for IHT.
- *Policy written in trust*: A life insurance policy with a trust arrangement attached, leaving the proceeds to named beneficiaries.
- *Power of appointment trust*: A trust which is flexible because beneficiaries can be added, and the proportion of the assets which existing beneficiaries are entitled to can be changed in the future. Discretionary trusts and flexible trusts come under this heading.
- *Simple trust*: See 'Absolute trust'.
- *Will trust*: A discretionary trust attached to a will, designed particularly to reduce liability to IHT.

The trusts for inheritance tax planning flowchart on the page opposite directs you to the types of trust that you can use if you want to achieve certain results: for example, providing an income.

> **EXAMPLE**
> You and your spouse have assets worth £600,000 divided equally between you. If one spouse dies leaving the other his or her £300,000, there's no IHT because gifts to spouses are exempt. But when the other spouse dies and leaves the whole £600,000 to the family, IHT will be payable on £385,000 (£600,000 less the £215,000 nil rate band). So, at 40% the tax bill would be £154,000. You need a clause in each will establishing a trust. The amount of the nil rate band, £215,000, goes into the trust.
>
> When the second spouse dies and the whole estate is left to the family, IHT of £68,000 will be payable on £170,000 – the second spouse's estate of £385,000 less her nil rate band.

Using trusts for inheritance tax planning

Is your estate likely to be worth more than the nil-rate band for IHT (currently £215,000)?

- **No** → **Do you want to pass assets on to someone other than a spouse?**
  - **Yes** → (proceeds to children/grandchildren question)
  - **No** → Ensure your will makes provision for the assets to pass to your spouse.

- **Yes** → **Do you want to pass assets on to a spouse?**
  - **Yes** → Consider a discretionary will trust.
  - **No** → **Do you want to pass assets on to children or grandchildren?**
    - **No** → Take further advice on trusts.
    - **Yes** → **Do you need to start making regular savings for children or grandchildren?**
      - **Yes** → Consider a bare trust.
      - **No** → **Do you know which children you want to pass assets to, and how much you want to give them?**
        - **No** → Consider a discretionary trust, but check the capital gains tax position.
        - **Yes** → **Do you want the beneficiaries to receive income?**
          - **Yes** → Consider an interest in possession trust, but check the capital gains tax position.
          - **No** → **Are the beneficiaries under 25?**
            - **No** → Consider a discretionary trust, but check the capital gains tax position.
            - **Yes** → Consider an accumulation and maintenance trust, but check the capital gains tax position.

Using life insurance to pay the bill

TERM INSURANCE IS USEFUL if you make a gift which could become taxable if you died within seven years. A whole life policy could pay out to cover IHT on something which you want to hang on to – you take out enough insurance to cover any potential tax bill.

You could take out life insurance to cover any likely tax bill on what you leave in your will, but you'll need to weigh up the cost against the potential tax saving. Life insurance figures prominently in off-the-peg estate planning schemes that are sold by financial advisers.

Putting plans into practice

A PROFESSIONAL WILL be able to establish how IHT affects the way your will should be written. It's not only important for ensuring people receive what you want them to receive, and that trust terms are incorporated where necessary, but also for indicating who will pay any IHT.

You might specify that certain bequests will be subject to tax, otherwise the tax may be taken out of what's left after most bequests are made and reduce what's available for your spouse, for example.

Trusts are usually drawn up by a solicitor. You can use the Law Society's *Solicitors Regional Directory* in your local library to find a firm which specialises in drawing up trusts. Specialists will be able to advise you on the most suitable trust – it is not easy to specify the type of trust you should go for and you need to make sure all the relevant details are taken into account.

It costs several hundred pounds to set up a trust and it can cost more than £100 a year to run, so you need to put enough into the trust to make the running costs worthwhile – the minimum would probably be £10,000.

Working out the value of your estate

IN WORKING OUT the value of your estate, remember to include your share of anything that is jointly owned.

The most obvious asset to take into consideration is property but others include:
- Investments such as bank and building society accounts, unit trusts and investment trusts, bonds, gilts, National Savings, shares and others.
- Valuables, including antiques and art.
- Gifts made in the last seven years.

If the total for all of the above were to come to more than £215,000, and you were to die in the tax year 1997/98, there would be inheritance tax to pay.

Action plan

- Work out the total value of what you own (on your own and your share of anything owned with others). You also need to add certain things you have given away in the last seven years. If it's more than or almost £215,000, then start thinking about IHT planning.

- Consider redistributing your wealth – remember there's no tax to pay when you transfer assets or investments to your spouse.

- Decide whether you want to reduce the value of what would be your estate by giving possessions or money away, but don't put yourself in financial difficulties to save your family a few thousand pounds in IHT.

- Get professional advice if you think you need to set up a trust – you need to put at least £10,000 in a trust if you are to make the running costs worthwhile.

- If you can't avoid the possibility of an IHT bill altogether, consider taking out life insurance to pay the bill.

TAX

10 Filling in your tax return

Not everyone receives a tax return. For example, if you are a basic-rate taxpayer, entitled only to the basic personal allowance, and you do not have any tax complications it is unlikely that you will receive one. But bear in mind that it is up to you to make sure the Inland Revenue knows about any income or gains, so if you don't get a tax return it is worth asking for one, or at the very least checking with the Inland Revenue.

The tax return covered in this chapter is the form for the 1996/97 tax year, so if you have not already completed yours, you can work through it using the next twenty or so pages. For ease of reference we've reproduced pages of the tax return on each left-hand page, with relevant guidance on the opposite, right-hand page.

As this book was published, there were rumours of a disaster waiting to happen as millions of people missed the 30 September deadline (see Chapter 3). The Inland Revenue said it wasn't worried. But if you're one of those who still hasn't sent the form back and you're not planning to work out the bill yourself, this chapter is a good place to start.

The new-style tax return consists of a basic eight-page form which everyone has to fill in, ten sets of supplementary pages, and a tax calculation guide. You need fill in only those supplementary pages which apply to you, and your tax office will send the ones which it thinks appropriate; if they do not apply to you, ignore them. However, it is your responsibility to ask for any pages not sent which you do need to fill in. The supplementary pages are:

○ Employment.
○ Share schemes.
○ Self-employment.
○ Partnership (two versions).
○ Land and property.

- Foreign.
- Trusts, etc.
- Capital gains.
- Non-residence.

You can obtain the supplementary pages by telephoning the Orderline on (0645) 000404. The Inland Revenue says four out of five taxpayers should have received a tax return which is the same length or shorter than the old form.

The tax calculation guide is available for people who want to work out their own tax bill, but you can leave the calculations up to your tax office if you wish. To ensure you get all the necessary supplementary pages, the second page of the basic form asks you a series of questions. For each question to which you answer yes you will need a supplementary page. We have not included the Partnership, Foreign, Trusts and Non-residence supplementary pages in this chapter. If these pages are relevant to you, you may find professional help useful.

Everyone who is sent a tax return should receive a tax return guide with explanatory notes for all the return pages. There are also new help sheets, designed to help you fill out specific parts of the new tax return. These contain step-by-step working sheets to help you calculate exactly what figures you need to put on the tax return. They are available on request by ringing the Orderline.

First, fill in the supplementary pages, and then fill in the basic form; sign and date the declaration and fill in question 18 if you have calculated your own tax bill. This chapter runs in that order: supplementary pages first then the basic form.

It is a good idea to keep a photocopy of the form once you've filled it in, in case of any queries or in case you want to check the details you have given and amend any mistakes later. You will find additional information boxes throughout the tax return; use these if you need extra space to write down extra information, or to tell your tax office anything you are unsure about.

> Bear in mind this tax return relates to the 1996/97 tax year. Most of the rest of this book covers the rules for the 1997/98 tax year – some things have changed. For example the tax-free slice for capital gains tax was £6,300 for 1986/97 (£6,500 for 1997/8 – see Chapter 8). And the limit for the Rent-A-Room scheme was £3,250 for 1996/97 (£4,250 for 1997/98 – see Chapter 4).

Step-by-step guide to filling in your tax return

1. Read through the first couple of pages of the return to check you've got the right supplementary pages.

2. If you need further pages, call the Orderline.

3. Read through the form and relevant supplementary pages (along with this chapter) to identify the documents you need.

4. Gather together the relevant documents – you should try and keep these in one place if possible from now on.

5. Work through the form, starting with the supplementary pages.

6. Once the return is completed, take a copy and send it back in the window envelope provided.

WHERE TO GET HELP

You may be tempted to pay someone else to complete the return – just after the new returns were issued there was a plethora of advertisements for tax return services on offer from banks, accountants, and solicitors. 'Worried about self assessment? You have good reason to be!' was a typically misleading teaser in one of these ads. But most of the services offering to complete the return for £100 or less are offered only to people with uncomplicated tax affairs. It will probably take you some time to work out whether you're eligible – you might as well have done the form yourself in that time!

The Inland Revenue offers plenty of free advice. You can call your tax office, or drop in at the nearest Tax Enquiry Centre (see Chapter 3). Alternatively, you can phone the Helpline on 0645 000444. The Revenue won't fill the form in for you, but it can tell you where to put the figures if you're unsure.

If you just want to save time by paying someone else to do your paperwork, make sure all you have to do is provide documents. If you want extra help and your circumstances are outside the scope of the flat-fee services, check that your adviser has suitable qualifications and experience and get a quote for the work first.

All the tax returns on the following pages are reproduced by permission of the Inland Revenue.

Income for the year ended 5 April 1997

EMPLOYMENT

Inland Revenue

Name | **Tax reference**

Fill in these boxes first

If you want help, look up the box numbers in the Notes. If you are a minister of religion, fill in the Ministers of Religion Pages.

Details of employer

Employer's PAYE reference
1.1

Employer's name
1.2

Date employment started (only if between 6 April 1996 and 5 April 1997)
1.3 / /

Employer's address
1.5

Date finished (only if between 6 April 1996 and 5 April 1997)
1.4 / /

Postcode

Tick box 1.6 if you were a director of the company
1.6

and, if so, tick box 1.7 if it was a close company
1.7

Income from employment

■ *Money* - see Notes, page EN3

Before tax

- Payments from P60 (or P45 or pay slips) — **1.8** £

- Payments not on P60 etc
  - tips — **1.9** £
  - other payments (excluding expenses shown below and lump sums and compensation payments or benefits shown overleaf) — **1.10** £

Tax deducted

- Tax deducted from payments in boxes 1.8 to 1.10 — **1.11** £

■ *Benefits and expenses* - see Notes, pages EN3 to EN6

	Amount		Amount
• Assets transferred/ payments made for you	**1.12** £	• Vans	**1.18** £
• Vouchers/credit cards	**1.13** £	• Interest-free and low-interest loans	**1.19** £
• Living accommodation	**1.14** £	• Mobile telephones	**1.20** £
• Mileage allowance	**1.15** £	• Private medical or dental insurance	**1.21** £
• Company cars	**1.16** £	• Other benefits	**1.22** £
• Fuel for company cars	**1.17** £	• Expenses payments received and balancing charges	**1.23** £

SA101

BMSD 12/96 — TAX RETURN ■ EMPLOYMENT: PAGE E1 — *Please turn over*

Employment supplementary pages

YOU WILL NEED to fill in this section if you received income, taxable benefits, or lump-sum payments from employment in the UK or abroad. Fill in a separate copy of the employment page for each employer you had in the 1996/97 year.

DETAILS OF EMPLOYER
Your employer (or each employer you had on 5 April 1997, if you have more than one job) should have given you a form P60 by 31 May 1997 for the 1996/97 tax year. This form gives figures for your pay, including sick pay and maternity pay. If earnings from a previous employer are not included on your P60, look at form P45 (given when you left your previous job), or your old payslips.

INCOME FROM EMPLOYMENT

Money
1.8 Put your pre-tax pay from your P60, P45 or payslips. Your P60 pay figure should exclude items deducted from your pay on which you get tax relief – pension contributions for example.
1.9 Put value of tips, unless they have already been included in the figures on form P60, form P45 or payslips.
1.10 Put other cash payments. Exclude expenses, lump sums, and compensation.
1.11 Put tax deducted (or tax refunded in brackets).

Benefits and expenses
Your employer should have given you form P11D by 6 July 1997. This gives details of expenses paid to you and perks, such as company cars. Check the figures and sort out with your employer any amounts that you think are wrong. Include details of expenses paid these will not be taxed if you can claim them as allowable expenses in boxes **1.32** to **1.35**.

147

Income from employment continued

Lump sums and compensation payments or benefits

You must read page EN6 of the Notes and fill in Help Sheet IR204 **before** filling in boxes 1.24 to 1.30

Reliefs

- £30,000 exemption — 1.24 £
- Foreign service and disability — 1.25 £
- Retirement and death lump sums — 1.26 £

Taxable lump sums

- From box H of *Help Sheet IR204* — 1.27 £
- From box Q of *Help Sheet IR204* — 1.28 £
- From box R of *Help Sheet IR204* — 1.29 £

Tax deducted
- Tax deducted from payments in boxes 1.27 to 1.29 — 1.30 £

Foreign earnings not taxable in the UK in year ended 5 April 1997 - see Notes, page EN6 — 1.31 £

Expenses you incurred in doing your job - see Notes, page EN7

- Travel and subsistence costs — 1.32 £
- Fixed deductions for expenses — 1.33 £
- Professional fees and subscriptions — 1.34 £
- Other expenses and capital allowances — 1.35 £
- Tick box 1.36 if the figure in box 1.32 includes travelling from home to work — 1.36

Foreign Earnings Deduction — 1.37 £

Foreign tax for which tax credit relief not claimed — 1.38 £

Additional information

*Now fill in any other supplementary Pages that apply to you.
Otherwise, go back to page 2 in your Tax Return and finish filling it in.*

BMSD 12/96   TAX RETURN ■ EMPLOYMENT: PAGE E2

Printed in the UK by St Ives Direct, St Ives plc. W0H2347 2/97.

Employment supplementary pages continued

Lump sums and compensation payments or benefits
Here you put details of lump sum payments from your employer for redundancy, for example.

RELIEFS
1.24 Put the tax-free portion, of up to £30,000, of any redundancy payment – see the working sheet on help sheet IR204.
1.25 Put the amount of lump sum payment which relates to a period when you were working abroad and did not have to pay UK tax on your earnings. See help sheet IR204.
1.26 Put the amount you have received or had paid into from an unapproved pension scheme. (Most schemes are approved.)

TAXABLE LUMP SUMS
See the relevant working sheets to see if you need to fill this in.

Foreign earnings not taxable in the UK
Put the amount of earnings from employment abroad which are not liable to UK income tax, using help sheet IR211.

EXPENSES YOU INCURRED IN DOING YOUR JOB
Here you include money you've paid out in the course of doing your job. You don't include expenses for which you've been reimbursed by your employer (unless these aren't covered by a dispensation for your employer – check if you're not sure).

Foreign earnings deduction
Put the amount of any earnings from working abroad that you don't have to pay tax on if you qualify for the foreign earnings deduction (see Chapter 5).

Foreign tax for which tax credit relief not claimed
Put the amount of foreign tax you've paid, or leave blank, and claim relief on the Foreign supplementary pages (not covered in this book).

Income for the year ended 5 April 1997

SHARE SCHEMES

Inland Revenue

Fill in these boxes first

Name

Tax reference

If you want help, look up the box numbers in the Notes.

Share options

Read the Notes, pages SN1 to SN4 before filling in the boxes

■ Approved savings-related share options

	Name of company (2.1/2.4)	Tick if shares unlisted (2.2/2.5)	Taxable amount (2.3/2.6)
• Exercise	2.1	2.2	2.3 £
• Cancellation or release	2.4	2.5	2.6 £

■ Approved discretionary share options

	Name of company	Tick if shares unlisted	Taxable amount
• Exercise	2.7	2.8	2.9 £
• Cancellation or release	2.10	2.11	2.12 £

■ Unapproved share options

	Name of company	Tick if shares unlisted	Taxable amount
• Grant	2.13	2.14	2.15 £
• Exercise	2.16	2.17	2.18 £
• Cancellation or release	2.19	2.20	2.21 £

Shares acquired

Read the Notes, page SN4 before filling in the boxes

	Name of company		Taxable amount
• Shares received from your employment	2.22	2.23	2.24 £
• Shares as benefits	2.25	2.26	2.27 £
• Post-acquisition charges	2.28	2.29	2.30 £

• Total of the taxable amounts boxes (boxes 2.3 to 2.30) — *total column above* — 2.31A £

• Any taxable amounts included in boxes 2.18 or 2.24 which are on your P60 or P45(Part 1A) — 2.31B £

Total taxable amount — *box 2.31A minus box 2.31B* — 2.31 £

Additional information

SA102

BMSD 12/96 TAX RETURN ■ SHARE SCHEMES: PAGE S1

Share schemes supplementary pages

YOU WILL NEED to fill in this section if you benefited from shares (or an interest in shares) through your employment and the benefit gives rise to tax (in many cases there is no tax to pay).

SHARE OPTIONS
More employees are now being given the chance to take part in schemes giving them shares in their employing firm. There are various types of schemes, and those approved by the Inland Revenue carry tax breaks. If your scheme is approved, you will not usually be taxed on the value of free shares you receive, the value of an option to buy shares at a favourable price, or the buying of shares using an option. However, there are cases where there may be tax to pay on shares you acquire, even in approved schemes. Your employer can tell you the type of scheme you are in, whether it is approved, and the shares market value. Tick the relevant boxes if the shares are unquoted – if you are unsure, ask your employer.

SHARES ACQUIRED
2.22–2.24 You may simply be given free or cheap shares as a perk.
2.25–2.27 You may have acquired shares or partly paid shares, and paid in instalments.
2.28–2.30
- You may have received shares through work which rose in value after you acquired them because of an alteration in special rights you had that came with the shares or because there was a change in restrictions to the shares (or to other shares in the company). For example, a restriction that employees cannot receive dividends from their shares might be lifted which could lead to a rise in the value of your shares.
- You may have received shares in a company which was a dependent subsidiary or which has become one.
- You may have received benefits as a result of owning shares, for example bonus shares or vouchers you can exchange for services.

2.31 Put the total of boxes **2.3** to **2.30** here.

You must complete a separate copy of this Page for each taxable event in the year ended 5 April 1997 that relates to your share options or shares acquired. If you had more than one taxable event in the year, either photocopy this Page or ask the Orderline for more copies, or photocopy this Page. (If you use a photocopy, please put your name and tax reference at the top.)

Share options

Read the Notes, pages SN2 to SN4 before filling in the boxes

Name of company
- 2.32

Class of share (for example, 10p Ordinary)
- 2.33

	Grant	Exercise	Cancellation/Release
2.34 Date option was granted	/ /	/ /	/ /
2.35 Date option was exercised		/ /	
2.36 Number of shares			
2.37 Exercise price/option price per share	£ .	£ .	
2.38 Amount paid for option	£ .	£ .	£ .
2.39 Market value per share at date the option was granted	£ .		
2.40 Market value per share at date the option was exercised		£ .	
2.41 Amount received in money or money's worth			£ .

Shares acquired

Read the Notes, page SN5 before filling in the boxes

Name of company
- 2.42

Class of share (for example, 10p Ordinary)
- 2.43

	Shares acquired	Post-acquisition charge
2.44 Date shares acquired	/ /	/ /
2.45 Number of shares		
2.46 Amount paid per share	£ .	
2.47 Market value per share at date of acquisition	£ .	£ .
2.48 Give details of the nature of the post-acquisition event		

BMSD 12/96

Share schemes supplementary pages continued

SHARE OPTIONS AND SHARES ACQUIRED
2.32–2.48 If you have to pay tax for more than one occasion in the tax year which gives rise to a tax bill, complete a copy of page S2 of the share schemes pages for each occasion. You have to fill in page S1 only once to cover all occasions.

Approved profit-sharing schemes
These are schemes where you are given free shares, depending on the profits of the company. Initially, the free shares are held in trust for you; if you do not keep the shares in trust for three years there could be tax to pay, but you put details on the employment supplementary pages.

Working out the taxable amounts
The explanatory notes help you establish the taxable amounts – there are different rules according to what you have done. For example, if you exercise an option or are given free or cheap shares as a perk, you will be taxed on the difference between what you paid for the shares (if anything) and their market value on the day you bought them; if you cancel or release an option, you will be taxed on the cash or value you receive; if you were given or granted an option, you will be taxed on the value of the option and if you received shares through work which rose in value after you acquired them because of an alteration in special rights or restrictions, you will be taxed on their rise in value. Check the explanatory notes if you paid for shares in instalments.

When all shares are taxed
Once shares from any scheme – approved or unapproved – are yours, they are treated like any other shares. Dividends are taxable and if you dispose of the shares for more than their value when you acquired them, the gain is liable to capital gains tax. Income tax on share dividends and capital gains tax on gains are dealt with in other parts of the tax return. Do not give details on the share schemes supplementary pages.

Income for the year ended 5 April 1997

SELF-EMPLOYMENT

Inland Revenue

Name | Tax reference

Fill in these boxes first

Read pages SEN1 and SEN2 before you start to fill in these Pages: there are special rules for the year ended 5 April 1997, and you may need to complete more than one set of Pages. If you were a Name at Lloyd's, fill in the Lloyd's Underwriters Pages instead.

Business details

Name of business — **3.1**

Description of business — **3.2**

Address of business — **3.3**

Postcode

Accounting period - *read the Notes, page SEN2 before filling in these boxes*

Start **3.4** / /   End **3.5** / /

- Tick this box if details in boxes 3.1 or 3.3 have changed since your last Tax Return **3.6**

- Tick box 3.7 if your accounts do not cover the period from the last accounting date (explain why in the 'Additional information' box below) **3.7**

- Date of commencement if after 5 April 1994 **3.9** / /

- Tick box 3.8 if you wish voluntarily to disclose that you have applied the anti-avoidance rules in Schedule 22 FA 1995 when calculating your profits for 1996-97 **3.8**

- Date of cessation if before 6 April 1997 **3.10** / /

Additional information

Income and expenses - annual turnover below £15,000

If your annual turnover is £15,000 or more, **ignore** boxes 3.11 to 3.13.   *Now fill in Page SE2*

If your annual turnover is below £15,000, **fill in boxes 3.11 to 3.13 instead of Page SE2**. Read the Notes, page SEN2.

- Turnover, other business receipts and goods etc. taken for personal use — **3.11** £

- Expenses allowable for tax — **3.12** £

box 3.11 *minus* box 3.12

Net profit (put figure in brackets if a loss) — **3.13** £

Now fill in Page SE3

SA103

BMSD 12/96   TAX RETURN ■ SELF-EMPLOYMENT: PAGE SE1

Self-employment supplementary pages

You will need to fill in this section if you have income from self-employment, which could include freelance earnings on top of the income from your main employment. Income from letting property may count as a trade

If you became self-employed before 6 April 1994, you were taxed on a preceding year basis in 1995/96 and will be taxed on a current year basis in 1997/98. The 1996/97 tax year counts as a transitional year. Basically, you will be taxed on half of your profits covering two years, so you may have to provide details here for two accounting years. If you became self-employed after 6 April 1994, you will have been taxed on a current year basis from the start.

If your tax basis period includes more than one accounting period, fill in a separate copy of the self-employment pages for each period (unless your turnover is less than £15,000). If you are involved in more than one business, fill in a separate copy of the self-employment pages for each one. If you are in a partnership, you fill in the Partnership supplementary pages instead (not covered in this book).

You do not need to send in your accounts with your tax return, but you do need to keep any paperwork which supports your tax return in case your tax office wants to delve further. Self-employed people have to keep documents relating to the 1996/97 tax year until 31 January 2003.

Income and expenses
3.11–3.13 If your turnover is less than £15,000, you can simply enter three figures for your turnover, allowable expenses, and net profit (which is turnover less your expenses). You can then go straight to the third page of the self-employment pages.

Income and expenses - annual turnover £15,000 or more

You must fill in this Page if your annual turnover is £15,000 or more - read the Notes, page SEN2

If you were registered for VAT, do the figures in boxes 3.16 to 3.51, include VAT? **3.14** ☐ or exclude VAT? **3.15** ☐

Sales/business income (turnover) **3.16** £ _____

	Disallowable expenses included in boxes 3.33 to 3.50	Total expenses
• Cost of sales	3.17 £	3.33 £
• Construction industry subcontractor costs	3.18 £	3.34 £
• Other direct costs	3.19 £	3.35 £

box 3.16 *minus* (box 3.33 + box 3.34 + box 3.35)

Gross profit/(loss) **3.36** £ _____

Other income/profits **3.37** £ _____

• Employee costs	3.20 £	3.38 £
• Premises costs	3.21 £	3.39 £
• Repairs	3.22 £	3.40 £
• General administrative expenses	3.23 £	3.41 £
• Motor expenses	3.24 £	3.42 £
• Travel and subsistence	3.25 £	3.43 £
• Advertising, promotion and entertainment	3.26 £	3.44 £
• Legal and professional costs	3.27 £	3.45 £
• Bad debts	3.28 £	3.46 £
• Interest	3.29 £	3.47 £
• Other finance charges	3.30 £	3.48 £
• Depreciation and loss/(profit) on sale	3.31 £	3.49 £
• Other expenses	3.32 £	3.50 £

Put the total of boxes 3.17 to 3.32 in box 3.53 below

total of boxes 3.38 to 3.50

Total expenses **3.51** £ _____

boxes 3.36 + 3.37 *minus* box 3.51

Net profit/(loss) **3.52** £ _____

Tax adjustments to net profit or loss

• Disallowable expenses

total of boxes 3.17 to 3.32
3.53 £ _____

• Goods etc. taken for personal use and other adjustments (apart from disallowable expenses) that increase profits
3.54 £ _____

box 3.53 + box 3.54

Total additions to net profit (deduct from net loss) **3.55** £ _____

• Deductions from net profit (add to net loss) **3.56** £ _____

boxes 3.52 + 3.55 *minus* box 3.56

Net business profit for tax purposes (put figure in brackets if a loss) **3.57** £ _____

BMSD 12/96   TAX RETURN ■ SELF-EMPLOYMENT: PAGE SE2   Now fill in Page SE3 ▶

Self-employment supplementary pages continued

INCOME AND EXPENSES

If you have completed the bottom of the previous page because your turnover was less than £15,000, you can ignore this page.

3.14–3.15 How you complete this section depends on whether or not you're registered for VAT, see Chapter 5.

3.16 Put your turnover – the money that has come in, excluding enterprise allowance or business start-up allowance.

3.33–3.35 Put the relevant allowable expenses.

3.36 Put an amount for your gross profit (or loss). This is the turnover figure in box **3.16** less the amounts in **3.33** to **3.35**.

3.37 Put any income from your business which has not been included in the turnover figure given at box **3.16** – for example interest earned on a business bank account.

3.38–3.50 Put the allowable expenses you are claiming.

3.51 Put the total of all the expenses you have listed in boxes **3.38** to **3.50**, but do not include the expenses in boxes **3.33** to **3.35**.

3.52 Put your net profit or loss – your gross profit and other income (boxes **3.36** and **3.37**), less the expenses total in box **3.51**.

3.17–3.32 These boxes are for any part of your expenses that you cannot claim as an allowable expense but which have been included in the boxes on the right-hand side (**3.33** to **3.50**). For example, you can claim as an expense the fees your accountant charges for preparing your business accounts, but not for any part of the accountants bill which relates to general personal financial advice.

TAX ADJUSTMENTS TO NET PROFIT OR LOSS

3.53 Put the total of all the disallowed expenses (**3.17** to **3.32**).

3.54 Put the value of anything you have taken out of the business for non-business (or personal) use.

3.55 Put the total of disallowed expenses and items taken out of the business from boxes **3.53** and **3.54**.

3.56 Put the amount (if anything) that needs to be deducted from your taxable profits.

3.57 Take your net profit in box **3.52**, add the total in box **3.55**, then take away the amount in **3.56**.

You must fill in this Page (leave blank any boxes that do not apply to you)

Capital allowances - summary

	Capital allowances	Balancing charge
• Motor cars (Separate calculations must be made for each motor car costing more than £12,000 and for cars used partly for private motoring.)	3.58 £	3.59 £
• Other business plant and machinery	3.60 £	3.61 £
• Agricultural or Industrial Buildings Allowance (A separate calculation must be made for each block of expenditure.)	3.62 £	3.63 £
• Other capital allowances claimed (Separate calculations must be made.)	3.64 £	3.65 £
	total of column above	total of column above
Total capital allowances/balancing charges	3.66 £	3.67 £

Adjustments to arrive at taxable profit or loss

Basis period begins 3.68 / /   and ends 3.69 / /

Read the Notes, page SEN3 - your basis period may be longer than your accounting period

Did your business start before 6 April 1994? - *Important: tick either the 'Yes' box or the 'No' box below*

Yes ☐   No ☐

If 'Yes', complete this column   *If 'No', complete this column*

Profit from box 3.13 or box 3.57 (if loss, enter '0') 3.70 £

You may need to adjust the figure in box 3.70 to arrive at your 1996-97 taxable profit. Read the Notes, page SEN6. if you need more help, ask the Orderline for *Help Sheet IR230: Transitional rules for old businesses*

Adjusted profits for 1996-97 (if the adjustments result in a loss, enter '0') 3.71 £

Adjustment for farmers' averaging (show reductions in brackets) 3.72 £

from box 3.67
Add balancing charge 3.73 £

from box 3.66
Deduct capital allowances 3.74 £

Profit or loss from box 3.13 or box 3.57 3.75 £

from box 3.67
Add balancing charge 3.76 £

from box 3.66
Deduct capital allowances 3.77 £

Adjustment to arrive at profit or loss for this basis period 3.78 £

Adjustment for farmers' averaging (show reductions in brackets) 3.79 £

Net profit for 1996-97 (if loss, enter '0') 3.80 £

Allowable loss for 1996-97 3.81 £

• Loss offset against other income for 1996-97 3.82 £

• Loss to carry back 3.83 £

• Loss to carry forward (that is allowable loss not claimed in any other way) 3.84 £

• Losses brought forward from last year 3.85 £

• Losses brought forward from last year used this year 3.86 £

box 3.80 *minus* box 3.86
Taxable profit after losses brought forward 3.87 £

• Any other business income (for example, Enterprise Allowance (Business Start-up Allowance) received in 1996-97) 3.88 £

box 3.87 + box 3.88
Total taxable profits from this business 3.89 £

Please turn over

Self-employment supplementary pages continued

CAPITAL ALLOWANCES SUMMARY
You can claim allowances for items of capital expenditure such as buildings, machinery, vehicles, patents and so on. Basically, you can claim up to 25% of your capital expenditure in the 1996/97 tax year, plus 25% of your unclaimed pool of capital expenditure from previous years. What you put on this page depends on whether you started in business before 6 April 1994. If you did start before then, you should read the help sheet on transitional rules carefully before putting your figures down.

3.58–3.67 Put the amount you are claiming for capital allowances in boxes **3.58**, **3.60**, **3.62**, and **3.64**, and the total in **3.66**. Boxes **3.59**, **3.61**, **3.63**, **3.65**, and **3.67** are for balancing charges, see Chapter 5. If you started in business before 6 April 1994 and are filling in the self-employment pages for two different accounting periods, fill in boxes **3.58** to **3.67** only for your most recent accounting period. If you started in business after that date, fill in these boxes for each set of accounts.

ADJUSTMENTS TO ARRIVE AT TAXABLE PROFIT OR LOSS
You may have to complete more than one set of self-employment pages for different accounting periods, but you need to fill out this section only once (or once for each business, if you are involved in more than one business). There are boxes in this section which only farmers need pay attention to. You need to bring together the information from the previous pages as indicated. And refer to Help Sheet 230 if you need to make adjustments for the transitional period.

If you've made a loss and wish to use it to set it against other income for 1996/97, you need to indicate this in box **3.82**. If you want to use the loss to reduce a tax bill for previous years put the relevant amount in box **3.83**. Otherwise, indicate that the loss or any amount left over, after setting against other income or previous tax bills, is to be carried forward. If you've made a profit this year, but have made losses in the past, you can claim them in boxes **3.84** or **3.85** (see Chapter 5).

Class 4 National Insurance Contributions

- Tick this box if exception or deferment applies **3.90** ☐
- Adjustments to profit chargeable to Class 4 National Insurance Contributions **3.91** £
- Class 4 National Insurance Contributions due **3.92** £

Subcontractors in the construction industry

- Deductions made by contractors on account of tax (you must send your SC60s to us) and any other tax deducted from trading income. **3.93** £

Summary of balance sheet

Leave these boxes blank if you do not have a balance sheet

Assets
- Plant, machinery and motor vehicles **3.94** £
- Other fixed assets (premises, goodwill, investments etc.) **3.95** £
- Stock and work in progress **3.96** £
- Debtors/prepayments/other current assets **3.97** £
- Bank/building society balances **3.98** £
- Cash in hand **3.99** £

total of boxes 3.94 to 3.99 **3.100** £

Liabilities
- Trade creditors/accruals **3.101** £
- Loans and overdrawn bank accounts **3.102** £
- Other liabilities **3.103** £

total of boxes 3.101 to 3.103 **3.104** £

- Net business assets (put the figure in brackets if you had net business liabilities)

box 3.100 *minus* box 3.104 **3.105** £

Net business assets represented by

Capital Account
- Balance at start of period* **3.106** £
- Net profit/(loss)* **3.107** £
- Capital introduced **3.108** £
- Drawings **3.109** £

total of boxes 3.106 to 3.108 *minus* box 3.109 **3.110** £

- Balance at end of period*

*If the Capital Account is overdrawn, or the business made a net loss, show the figure in brackets.

Additional information

*Now fill in any other supplementary Pages that apply to you.
Otherwise, go back to Page 2 of your Tax Return and finish filling it in.*

BMSD 12/96 TAX RETURN ■ SELF-EMPLOYMENT: PAGE SE4

Self-employment supplementary pages continued

Class 4 National Insurance contributions
3.90 Tick if you don't have to pay Class 4 National Insurance contributions, and say why in the additional information box. If you tick box **3.90**, put a zero in boxes **3.91** and **3.92**.
3.91 Put the amount of your profits on which Class 4 National Insurance contributions have to be paid.
3.92 Put the amount of National Insurance due if you are calculating your own tax bill. Otherwise, leave blank.

Subcontractors in the construction industry
Form SC60, given to workers in the construction industry if they receive payments under the construction industry tax deduction scheme, should be sent to your tax office with your tax return.

Summary of balance sheet
Leave the boxes in this section (**3.94** to **3.110**) blank if you don't have a balance sheet or if your turnover was less than £15,000. Otherwise you need to enter amounts for your assets and liabilities. Assets include things like property and equipment and liabilities include debts, overdrafts and loans. Then you work out your net position – by deducting the liabilities from the assets.

Net business assets represented by capital account
3.106 Put your net assets (or net liabilities in brackets) at the start of the period.
3.107 Put your net profit (or loss in brackets). This should be the same as the amount you put in box **3.52**.
3.108 Put the total of capital introduced to the business during 1996/97.
3.109 Put the total of withdrawals from the business during 1996/97.
3.110 Put the balance at the end of the period by adding together the amounts in boxes **3.106** to **3.108** and deducting the amount in box **3.109**. Put a minus amount in brackets. You should have the same figure as you have given in box **3.105**.

Income for the year ended 5 April 1997

Inland Revenue — LAND AND PROPERTY

Fill in these boxes first

Name

Tax reference

If you want help, look up the box numbers in the Notes.

Are you claiming Rent a Room relief for gross rents of £3,250 or less?
(Or £1,625 if the claim is shared?) Read the Notes on page LN2 to find out how to claim relief for gross rents over £3,250. No ☐ Yes ☐

If 'Yes', and this is your only income from UK property, you have finished these Pages

Is your income from furnished holiday lettings?
If 'No', turn over and fill in Page L2 to give details of your property income. No ☐ Yes ☐

If 'Yes', fill in boxes 5.1 to 5.18 before completing Page L2

Furnished holiday lettings

- Income from furnished holiday lettings — **5.1** £ _____

■ *Expenses* (furnished holiday lettings only)

- Rent, rates, insurance, ground rents etc — **5.2** £ _____
- Repairs, maintenance and renewals — **5.3** £ _____
- Finance charges, including interest — **5.4** £ _____
- Legal and professional costs — **5.5** £ _____
- Cost of services provided, including wages — **5.6** £ _____
- Other expenses — **5.7** £ _____

total of boxes 5.2 to 5.7
5.8 £ _____

box 5.1 *minus* box 5.8

Net profit (put figures in brackets if a loss) — **5.9** £ _____

■ *Tax adjustments*

- Private use — **5.10** £ _____
- Balancing charges — **5.11** £ _____

box 5.10 + box 5.11
5.12 £ _____

- Capital allowances — **5.13** £ _____

boxes 5.9 + 5.12 *minus* box 5.13

Profit for the year (copy to box 5.19). If loss, enter '0' in box 5.14 and put the loss in box 5.15 — **5.14** £ _____

boxes 5.9 + 5.12 *minus* box 5.13

Loss for the year (if you have entered '0' in box 5.14) — **5.15** £ _____

- Loss offset against 1996-97 total income — **5.16** £ _____

see Notes, page LN4
- Loss carried back — **5.17** £ _____

see Notes, page LN4
- Loss offset against other income from property (copy to box 5.38) — **5.18** £ _____

SA105

BMSD 12/96   TAX RETURN ■ LAND AND PROPERTY: PAGE L1   *Please turn over*

Land and property supplementary pages

You will need to fill in these pages if you take in a lodger, receive rent or other income from land and property, receive taxable premiums from leases or get income from holiday lettings in the UK.

Exclude income you received from furnished accommodation in your only or main home which amounts to a trade, property abroad, property which comes from a partnership, waterways, mines, markets and fairs, tolls and bridges.

If you share the income with one or more other people: tick box **5.47** and put the name and address of the person who keeps the accounts in the additional information box on page 8 of the main tax return, put only your share of income and expenses on the Land and property supplementary pages, put only your share of the profit if you receive the income after expenses have been deducted, and leave the expenses boxes blank.

Are you claiming Rent-a-Room relief?
Tick yes if you want to claim tax relief for all your rental income, if it does not exceed £3,250 in the 1996/97 tax year and is covered by the Rent-a-Room scheme (see Chapter 4).

Is your income from furnished holiday lettings?
Tick yes if some or all of your income is from furnished holiday lettings. Or tick no and go to the next land and property page.

Furnished holiday lettings
5.1 Put the amount of income, including money you received for the provision of services.
5.2–5.18 The rest of this page is similar to the second Self Employment supplementary page. You need to include your expenses from your furnished holiday lettings – mortgage interest, and repair costs for example. Then, if necessary, you need to make adjustments to take account of any personal use. You can also claim for capital allowances and adjust any profit using losses made in previous years.

Other property income

■ Income

	copy from box 5.14	
• Furnished holiday lettings profits	5.19 £	
		Tax deducted
• Rents and other income from land and property	5.20 £	5.21 £
		boxes 5.19 + 5.20 + 5.22
• Chargeable premiums	5.22 £	5.23 £

■ Expenses (do not include figures you have already put in boxes 5.2 to 5.7 on Page L1)

• Rent, rates, insurance, ground rents etc	5.24 £	
• Repairs, maintenance and renewals	5.25 £	
• Finance charges, including interest	5.26 £	
• Legal and professional costs	5.27 £	
• Costs of services provided, including wages	5.28 £	total of boxes 5.24 to 5.29
• Other expenses	5.29 £	5.30 £

Net profit (put figures in brackets if a loss)
box 5.23 minus box 5.30
5.31 £

■ Tax adjustments

• Private use	5.32 £	
• Balancing charges	5.33 £	box 5.32 + box 5.33
		5.34 £
• Rent a Room exempt amount	5.35 £	
• Capital allowances	5.36 £	
• 10% wear and tear	5.37 £	total of boxes 5.35 to 5.38
• Furnished holiday lettings losses (from box 5.18)	5.38 £	5.39 £

Adjusted profit (if loss enter '0' in box 5.40 and put the loss in box 5.41)
boxes 5.31 + 5.34 minus box 5.39
5.40 £

Adjusted loss (if you have entered '0' in box 5.40)
boxes 5.31 + 5.34 minus box 5.39
5.41 £

• Loss brought forward from previous year 5.42 £

Profit for year
box 5.40 minus box 5.42
5.43 £

• Loss offset against total income 5.44 £

• Loss to carry forward to following year 5.45 £

• Pooled expenses from 'one estate election' carried forward 5.46 £

Tick box 5.47 if these pages include details of property let jointly 5.47

Now fill in any other supplementary Pages that apply to you.
Otherwise, go back to page 2 of your Tax Return and finish filling it in.

BMSD 12/96   TAX RETURN ■ LAND AND PROPERTY: PAGE L2

Printed in the UK by St Ives Direct, St Ives plc. W0H2355 2/97.

Land and property supplementary pages continued

OTHER PROPERTY INCOME
If you have an income from land or property you have a rental business even if your business amounts to little more than renting out your holiday home to friends. On this page you round up all the information about your land or property-letting activity.

Income
5.19 If you have income from furnished holiday lettings, put the amount from box **5.14** on the previous page.
5.20 Put the pre-tax amount of all your income from land and property except income from furnished holiday lettings (which goes in **5.19**) and chargeable premiums (which go in **5.22**).
5.21 If tax has been deducted from your rent before you received it, put the amount of tax deducted here (and include the pre-tax amount in box **5.20**).
5.22 Put the taxable amount of premiums for granting a lease of up to 50 years, and other payments received.
5.23 Put the total of boxes **5.19**, **5.20** and **5.22**.

Expenses
If your income before expenses is less than £15,000, ignore boxes **5.24** to **5.28**, and put all your expenses as one amount in box **5.29**. Otherwise, go through the list and put in the expenses you want to claim for your lettings other than furnished holiday lettings. Then, you can work out your net profit.

Tax adjustments
As before, you may need to adjust those expenses for any personal use. You may be able to claim capital allowances for equipment you own and you need to decide whether to opt for the actual cost of replacing furniture, or 10% of the net rent (see Chapter 4). Once you've made these adjustments, you may have losses from previous years to set against the profit. If you've made a loss overall, you need to decide whether you want it set against your total income or carried forward.

For the year ended 5 April 1997

CAPITAL GAINS

Inland Revenue

Fill in these boxes first

Name

Tax reference

If you want help, look up the box numbers in the Notes.

Chargeable gains and allowable losses

- Total chargeable gains for 1996-97 — **8.1** £

  minus Total allowable losses for 1996-97 — **8.2** £

  equals Net chargeable gains for 1996-97 — **8.3** £

  or equals Net allowable losses for 1996-97 — **8.4** £

  minus Trading losses, losses from furnished holiday lettings, post-cessation expenditure, or post-employment deductions which can reduce chargeable gains — **8.5** £

  minus Allowable losses brought forward — **8.6** £

  box 8.3 *minus* (box 8.5 + box 8.6)
  equals Chargeable gains for 1996-97 — **8.7** £

  box 8.7 *minus* £6,300
  Your chargeable gains *minus* exempt amount — **8.8** £

- Additional liability in respect of offshore trusts — **8.9** £

Capital losses

Use this part of the Page to record your allowable losses

Earlier years' losses

- Unused losses of earlier years — **8.10** £

  from box 8.6
- Used this year — **8.11** £

  box 8.10 minus box 8.11
- Carried forward losses of 1995-96 and earlier years — **8.12** £

This year's losses

  from box 8.2
- Total — **8.13** £

- Used against gains — **8.14** £

- Used against earlier years' gains — **8.15** £

- Used against income — **8.16** £

  box 8.13 *minus* (box 8.14 + box 8.15 + box 8.16)
- Carried forward losses of 1996-97 — **8.17** £

Additional information

SA108

BMSD 12/96   TAX RETURN ■ CAPITAL GAINS: PAGE CG1   *Please turn over*

Capital gains supplementary pages

You will need to fill in these pages if you disposed of assets in 1996/97, such as shares, unit trusts, or a second home, and they were worth £12,600 or more, or if you made chargeable gains of £6,300 or more. Disposal can mean selling or making a gift, but gifts between husband and wife are not chargeable; they are tax free.

Capital gains are any gains you made in the 1996/97 tax year from disposing of assets. You may find that if you work through the explanatory notes, help sheets, and do the calculations for capital gains tax, you do not need to fill in the capital gains supplementary pages because your chargeable gains come to less than £6,300. You arrive at your chargeable gains after taking account of inflation, see Chapter 8. Even if there's no tax to pay, give details of assets worth more than £12,600 that you disposed of.

Your main home does not normally give rise to a tax bill and can be ignored when you work out whether the assets you have disposed of are worth more than £12,600. And many other things you sell like a car or computer can be ignored. But antiques and fine art could give rise to a tax bill.

Confusingly, the Inland Revenue asks you to fill in the second of the capital gains supplementary pages first. When you have completed the second page, turn back to the first page. Opposite, we show the first page of the two.

Chargeable gains and allowable losses
8.18.9 Put the amount of your total chargeable gains in box **8.1**, then take account of any losses in boxes **8.2** to **8.6** and put the chargeable gain after losses in **8.7**. Deduct the tax-free allowance of £6,300 and put the result in **8.8** (see explanatory note for **8.8**).

Capital losses
Earlier years' losses/This year's losses
8.10–8.17 Boxes **8.10** to **8.17** are a record of chargeable losses for future tax years. It's a good idea to keep a photocopy of this page for future reference.

INCOME for the year ended 5 April 1997

Q10 Did you receive any income from UK savings and investments? ☐ NO ☐ YES

If yes, fill in boxes 10.1 to 10.32 as appropriate. Include only your share from any joint savings and investments.

■ Interest

- Interest from UK banks, building societies and deposit takers

  - where **no tax** has been deducted

    Taxable amount
    10.1 £

  - where **tax has** been deducted

Amount after tax deducted	Tax deducted	Gross amount before tax
10.2 £	10.3 £	10.4 £

- Interest distributions from UK authorised unit trusts and open-ended investment companies (dividend distributions go below)

Amount after tax deducted	Tax deducted	Gross amount before tax
10.5 £	10.6 £	10.7 £

- National Savings (other than FIRST Option Bonds and the first £70 of interest from a National Savings Ordinary Account)

  Taxable amount
  10.8 £

- National Savings FIRST Option Bonds

Amount after tax deducted	Tax deducted	Gross amount before tax
10.9 £	10.10 £	10.11 £

- Other income from UK savings and investments (except dividends)

Amount after tax deducted	Tax deducted	Gross amount before tax
10.12 £	10.13 £	10.14 £

■ Dividends

- Dividends and other qualifying distributions from UK companies

Dividend/distribution	Tax credit	Dividend/distribution plus credit
10.15 £	10.16 £	10.17 £

- Dividend distributions from UK authorised unit trusts and open-ended investment companies

Dividend/distribution	Tax credit	Dividend/distribution plus credit
10.18 £	10.19 £	10.20 £

- Scrip dividends from UK companies

Dividend	Notional tax	Dividend plus notional tax
10.21 £	10.22 £	10.23 £

- Foreign income dividends from UK companies

Dividend	Notional tax	Dividend plus notional tax
10.24 £	10.25 £	10.26 £

- Foreign income dividend distributions from UK authorised unit trusts and open-ended investment companies

Dividend	Notional tax	Dividend plus notional tax
10.27 £	10.28 £	10.29 £

- Non-qualifying distributions and loans written off

	Notional tax	Taxable amount
10.30 £	10.31 £	10.32 £

BMSD 12/96   TAX RETURN: PAGE 3   *Please turn over* ▶

Tax return page 3: Income

You will need to fill in this page if you received taxable income from UK savings and investments, for example, taxable interest from a bank, building society, National Savings or other deposit-taker, gilts, loan stock, credit unions, certain annuities or taxable dividends from UK shares and investment trusts, or taxable distributions from unit trusts.

You don't need to say where your interest and investment income comes from, just give the amounts. If you are not sure how much interest you have earned, ask the bank or building society for interest statements and certificates of tax deducted. Vouchers that come with share dividends and unit trust distributions show the tax deducted.

Exclude:
- Tax-free income – for example, income from TESSAs, PEPs, and some National Savings investments.
- Interest and investment income from offshore and overseas sources (see foreign supplementary pages).
- Equalisation payments from unit trusts.
- Interest and investment income which arises as a result of a partnership (see partnership supplementary pages).

Include:
- Your share of the income from joint investments.
- Interest and investment income for your children under 18 if it is more than £100 arising from a gift from you.
- Cash or shares from a building society merger, conversion or take-over (see explanatory notes).
- Any interest paid on your current account.
- Any gross interest you have received. You may need to put in only half your interest if it comes from a source which began before 6 April 1994 (see explanatory notes).

Q10 Did you receive any income from UK savings and investments?

If you answer 'No' to **Q10**, go to **Q11**.
Otherwise check through the list **10.1** to **10.30** and include any amounts you received in the 1996/97 tax year.

INCOME for the year ended 5 April 1997, continued

Q11 Did you receive a UK pension, retirement annuity or Social Security benefit? NO ☐ YES ☐ *If yes, fill in boxes 11.1 to 11.13 as appropriate.*

■ **State pensions and benefits**

Taxable amount for 1996-97

- State Retirement Pension — **11.1** £
- Widow's Pension — **11.2** £
- Widowed Mother's Allowance — **11.3** £
- Industrial Death Benefit Pension — **11.4** £
- Unemployment Benefit, Income Support and Jobseeker's Allowance — **11.5** £
- Invalid Care Allowance — **11.6** £
- Statutory Sick Pay and Statutory Maternity Pay paid by the Department of Social Security — **11.7** £

	Tax deducted	Gross amount before tax
• Taxable Incapacity Benefit	**11.8** £	**11.9** £

■ **Other pensions and retirement annuities**

	Amount after tax deducted	Tax deducted	Gross amount before tax
• Pensions (other than State pensions) and retirement annuities	**11.10** £	**11.11** £	**11.12** £

- Exemption/deduction — *see notes in your Tax Return Guide*
  Exempt amount **11.13** £

Q12 Did you receive any of the following kinds of income? NO ☐ YES ☐ *If yes, fill in boxes 12.1 to 12.12 as appropriate*

	Income receivable	Exempt amount	Income less exempt amount
• Taxable maintenance or alimony	**12.1** £	**12.2** £	**12.3** £

	Number of years		Amount of gain
• Gains on UK life insurance policies (without notional tax)	**12.4**		**12.5** £

	Number of years	Notional tax	Amount of gain
• Gains on UK life insurance policies (with notional tax)	**12.6**	**12.7** £	**12.8** £

Amount
Corresponding deficiency relief **12.9** £

	Amount received	Notional tax	Amount plus notional tax
• Refunds of surplus additional voluntary contributions	**12.10** £	**12.11** £	**12.12** £

Q13 Did you receive any other income which you have not already entered elsewhere in your Tax Return? NO ☐ YES ☐ *If yes, fill in boxes 13.1 to 13.6 as appropriate*
Make sure you fill in any supplementary Pages before answering Question 13.

	Amount after tax deducted	Tax deducted	Amount before tax
• Other income	**13.1** £	**13.2** £	**13.3** £

	Losses brought forward	Losses used in 1996-97
	13.4 £	**13.5** £

Losses sustained in 1996-97 **13.6** £

BMSD 12/96   TAX RETURN: PAGE 4

Tax return page 4: Income
continued

You will need to fill in this page if you received taxable income from UK pensions and retirement annuities, taxable state benefits, taxable maintenance payments, taxable payouts from a life insurance policy, a refund of surplus additional coluntary contributions (AVCs), or any other taxable income not declared elsewhere.

If you answer 'No' to **Q11**, go straight to the next page.

State pensions and benefits
11.1 Put the amount of state pension you were entitled to for the 1996/97 tax year. This may be different from what you actually received if you were paid monthly or quarterly in arrears
11.2–11.9 This section is for any taxable benefits you received in 1996/97 or taxable sick or maternity pay. You should have a statement from your benefits office.

Other pensions and retirement annuities
11.10–11.12 Put details of UK (not foreign) pensions and annuities. Get the amounts from your form P60 (or other statement) provided by the payer of your pension. Include any income withdrawals from personal pensions
11.13 Put the exempt amount of certain pensions – part or all of pensions paid for illness, injury and disability are tax free.

Did you receive any of the following kinds of income?
Q12 If you answer 'No' go to **Q13**.
This section is a round-up of different types of income: maintenance payments, life insurance payouts and pension contributions refunds.

Did you receive any other income which you have not already entered elsewhere on your tax return?
Q13 If you answer 'No', move to **Q14**.
This is your last chance to tell the Revenue about any income you received, if you haven't found anywhere to put it so far. Include things like a cashback received if you took out a mortgage.

RELIEFS *for the year ended 5 April 1997*

Q14 ▸ Do you want to claim relief for pension contributions? NO ☐ YES ☐
Do not include contributions deducted from your pay by your employer, because tax relief is given automatically.

If yes, fill in boxes 14.1 to 14.17 as appropriate.

■ *Retirement annuity contracts*

Payments made in 1996-97	**14.1** £	1996-97 payments used in an earlier year	**14.2** £
1996-97 payments now to be carried back	**14.3** £	Payments brought back from 1997-98	**14.4** £

Relief claimed
box 14.1 *minus* (boxes 14.2 and 14.3, but not 14.4)
14.5 £

■ *Self-employed contributions to personal pension plans*

Payments made in 1996-97	**14.6** £	1996-97 payments used in an earlier year	**14.7** £
1996-97 payments now to be carried back	**14.8** £	Payments brought back from 1997-98	**14.9** £

Relief claimed
box 14.6 *minus* (boxes 14.7 and 14.8, but not 14.9)
14.10 £

■ *Employee contributions to personal pension plans* (include your gross contribution - *see the note on box 14.11 in your Tax Return Guide*)

Payments made in 1996-97	**14.11** £	1996-97 payments used in an earlier year	**14.12** £
1996-97 payments now to be carried back	**14.13** £	Payments brought back from 1997-98	**14.14** £

Relief claimed
box 14.11 *minus* (boxes 14.12 and 14.13, but not 14.14)
14.15 £

- Amount of contributions to employer's schemes **not deducted** at source from pay **14.16** £
- Gross amount of free-standing additional voluntary contributions paid in 1996-97 **14.17** £

Q15 ▸ Do you want to claim any of the following reliefs? NO ☐ YES ☐

If yes, fill in boxes 15.1 to 15.12, as appropriate.

- Payments you made for vocational training — Amount of payment **15.1** £
- Interest on loans to buy your main home (other than MIRAS) — Amount of payment **15.2** £
- Interest on other qualifying loans — Amount of payment **15.3** £
- Maintenance or alimony payments you have made under a court order, Child Support Agency assessment or legally binding order or agreement — Amount claimed under 'new' rules **15.4** £

  Amount claimed under 'old' rules up to £1,790 **15.5** £   Amount claimed under 'old' rules over £1,790 **15.6** £

- Subscriptions for Venture Capital Trust shares (up to £100,000) — Amount on which relief claimed **15.7** £
- Subscriptions under the Enterprise Investment Scheme (up to £100,000) — Amount on which relief claimed **15.8** £
- Charitable covenants or annuities — Amount of payment **15.9** £
- Gift Aid — Amount of payment **15.10** £
- Post-cessation expenses, and losses on relevant discounted securities — Amount of payment **15.11** £
- Payments to a trade union or friendly society for death benefits — Half amount of payment **15.12** £

BMSD 12/96   TAX RETURN: PAGE 5   *Please turn over* ▸

Tax return page 5: Reliefs

You will need to fill in this page if you want to claim tax relief for pension plans, vocational training, interest on loans, maintenance, venture capital trusts and the Enterprise Investment Scheme, donations to charity, expenses incurred after your business closed down, and certain trade-union and Friendly Society payments.

Give details of tax reliefs you are claiming for 1996/97. You do not need to claim for pension contributions deducted by your employer, but see box **14.16** if you have made a lump sum additional voluntary contribution payment.

Do you want to claim relief for pension contributions?
If you answer 'No' to **Q14**, go to **Q15**.
14.1, 14.6 and 14.11 Put the amount you paid into the relevant types of personal pension plan started before 1 July 1988.

Pension contributions paid in one tax year can be claimed as if paid in an earlier year. And you can carry forward unused tax relief from earlier tax years. **14.2** and/or **14.7** and/or **14.12** Put the amount already claimed in an earlier tax year. **14.3** and/or **14.8** and/or **14.13** Put the amount you want to carry back to an earlier tax year. **14.4** and/or **14.9** and/or **14.14** Put the amount paid after 5 April 1997 that you want to carry back to 1996/97. **14.5** and/or **14.10** and/or **14.15** Put the amount you are claiming, less the amounts for relief in earlier years.
14.16 Put the amount of lump sum additional voluntary contribution payments made to your employers scheme if you did not get tax relief through your employer.
14.17 Put the total amount you paid, plus the basic-rate tax relief the plan provider claimed, into free-standing additional voluntary contributions plans.

Do you want to claim any of the following reliefs?
If you answer 'No' to **Q15**, go to **Q16**.
15.1–15.12 In this section you need to include payments you made (other than to pensions or for a mortgage in MIRAS) for which you want to claim tax relief. Read through the list to see if you think any of them might apply and complete as indicated.

ALLOWANCES *for the year ended 5 April 1997*

Q16 You get your personal allowance of £3,765 automatically. If you were born before 6 April 1932, enter your date of birth in box 21.4 - you may get higher age-related allowances.

Do you want to claim any of the following allowances? NO ☐ YES ☐

If yes, please read pages 23 to 26 of your Tax Return Guide and then fill in boxes 16.1 to 16.28 as appropriate.

■ **Blind person's allowance**

- Date of registration (if first year of claim) **16.1** / /
- Local authority (or other register) **16.2**

■ **Transitional allowance** (for some wives with husbands on low income if received in earlier years).

- Tick to claim and give details in the 'Additional information' box on page 8 **16.3** ☐
  (please see page 23 of your Tax Return Guide for what is needed)
- If you want to calculate your tax, enter the amount of transitional allowance you can have in box 16.4 **16.4** £

■ **Married couple's allowance for a married man** - see page 23 of your Tax Return Guide.

- Wife's full name **16.5**
- Date of marriage (if after 5 April 1996) **16.6** / /
- Wife's date of birth (if before 6 April 1932) **16.7** / /
- Tick box 16.8 if you and your wife have allocated **half** the allowance to her **16.8** ☐
- Wife's tax reference (if known, please) **16.9**
- Tick box 16.10 if you and your wife have allocated **all** the allowance to her **16.10** ☐

■ **Married couple's allowance for a married woman** - see page 24 of your Tax Return Guide.

- Date of marriage (if after 5 April 1996) **16.11** / /
- Husband's full name **16.12**
- Tick box 16.13 if you and your husband have allocated **half** the allowance to you **16.13** ☐
- Husband's tax reference (if known, please) **16.14**
- Tick box 16.15 if you and your husband have allocated **all** the allowance to you **16.15** ☐

■ **Additional personal allowance** (available in some circumstances if you have a child living with you - see page 24 of your Tax Return Guide).

- Name of the child claimed for **16.16**
- Child's date of birth **16.17** / /
- Tick if child lives with you **16.18** ☐
- Name of university etc/type of training if the child is 16 or over on 6 April 1996 and in full time education or training **16.19**

Sharing a claim
Name and address of other person claiming
16.20

Postcode

- Enter your share as a percentage **16.21** %
- If share not agreed, enter the number of days in the year ended 5 April 1997 that the child lived with
  - you **16.22** days
  - other person **16.23** days

■ **Widow's bereavement allowance**
- Date of your husband's death **16.24** / /

■ **Transfer of surplus allowances** - see page 25 of your Tax Return Guide before you fill in boxes 16.25 to 16.28.

- Tick if you want your spouse to have your unused allowances **16.25** ☐
- Tick if you want to have your spouse's unused allowances **16.26** ☐

Please give details in the 'Additional information' box on page 8 - see page 25 of your Tax Return Guide for what is needed.
If you want to calculate your tax, enter the amount of the surplus allowance you can have.

- Blind person's surplus allowance **16.27** £
- Married couple's surplus allowance **16.28** £

BMSD 12/96 TAX RETURN: PAGE 6

Tax return page 6: Allowances

YOU WILL NEED to fill in this page if you want to claim blind person's allowance, married couple's allowance (and transitional allowance), additional personal allowance, widow's bereavement allowance, or if you want to transfer allowances to your spouse.

If you answer 'No' to **Q16**, go to **Q17**.

Blind person's allowance
Claim if you are registered blind in England and Wales. If you live in Northern Ireland or Scotland, claim if you are not able to perform any work for which eyesight is essential.

Transitional allowance
A married woman can claim transitional allowance (use any unused part of her husband's personal allowance) if she successfully claimed it in each tax year since 1990/91 and still qualifies.

Married couple's allowance
Claim if you were married and living with your spouse in 1996/97. It's too late to transfer it for 1996/97 and 1997/98.

Additional personal allowance
You can claim if you were single, separated, divorced or widowed and had a dependent child up to 16 years old (up to age 18 in some cases) for part of the tax year, or if you are a married man with a child, and your wife could not look after herself.

Widow's bereavement allowance
Put the date of your husband's death if he died during this tax year or the previous tax year if you didn't remarry by 5 April 1996.

Transfer of surplus allowances
16.25–16.26 Tick if you want to transfer any unused allowances to or from your spouse.
16.27–16.28 Fill in if you want to calculate your own tax bill.

OTHER INFORMATION for the year ended 5 April 1997

Q17 Have you had any 1996-97 tax refunded directly by your Tax Office or DSS Benefits Agency? **NO** / **YES**

If yes, enter the amount of the refund in box 17.1.

17.1 £

Q18 Do you want to calculate your tax? **NO** / **YES**

If yes, do it now and then fill in boxes 18.1 to 18.9. Your Tax Calculation Guide will help.

- Unpaid tax for earlier years included in your tax code for 1996-97 — 18.1 £
- Tax due for 1996-97 included in your tax code for a later year — 18.2 £
- Total tax due for 1996-97 *(put the amount in brackets if an overpayment)* — 18.3 £
- Tax due for earlier years — 18.4 £
- Tax overpaid for earlier years — 18.5 £
- Your first payment on account for 1997-98 — 18.6 £

Tick box 18.7 if you are making a claim to reduce your payments on account and say why in the 'Additional information' box 18.7

Tick box 18.8 if you do **not** need to make payments on account 18.8

- 1997-98 tax you are reclaiming now — 18.9 £

Q19 Do you want to claim a repayment if you have paid too much tax? **NO** / **YES**
(If you tick 'No', I will set any amount you are owed against your next tax bill.)

If yes, fill in boxes 19.1 to 19.12 as appropriate.

Should the repayment (or payment) be sent:

- to you? *(tick box 19.1 and go to Question 20)* 19.1

or

- to your bank or building society account or other nominee *(tick box 19.2 and fill in boxes 19.3 to 19.7 or boxes 19.3 to 19.12 as appropriate)*? 19.2

Please give details of your (or your nominee's) bank or building society account for repayment

Name of bank or building society 19.3
Branch sort code 19.4 — —
Account number 19.5
Name of account 19.6
Building society ref. 19.7

Fill in boxes 19.8 to 19.12 if you want the repayment to be made to someone other than yourself (a nominee).

Name
I authorise 19.8

If you want your repayment to be made to your agent tick box 19.9   19.9

Agent's ref. for you 19.10

Nominee's address 19.11

Postcode

to receive on my behalf the amount due

This authority must be signed by you. A photocopy of your signature will not do. 19.12

Signature

Q20 Are your details on the front of the Tax Return wrong? **NO** / **YES**

If yes, please make any corrections on the front of the form.

Q21 Please give other personal details in boxes 21.1 to 21.4

Please give a daytime telephone number if convenient. It is often simpler to phone if we need to ask you about your Tax Return.

Your telephone number 21.1

or, if you prefer, your agent's telephone number 21.2
(also give your agent's name and reference in the 'Additional information' box on page 8)

Say if you are single, married, widowed, divorced or separated 21.3

Date of birth 21.4 / /
Enter your date of birth if you were born before 6 April 1932, or you have ticked the 'Yes' box in Question 14, or you are claiming relief for Venture Capital Trust subscriptions

BMSD 12/96   TAX RETURN: PAGE 7   *Please turn over*

Tax return page 7: Other information

You'll need to fill in this page to confirm or amend the details on the front of the tax return, to give your marital status, to put your date of birth (if necessary), to give details of any refunds you have had or want to claim, to indicate that you want the Revenue to calculate your tax bill – or to put in the figures if you're doing it yourself

Have you had any 1996/97 tax refunded directly by your tax office or DSS Benefit Office?

If you answer 'No' to **Q17**, go to **Q18**. Otherwise, put the amount of tax refunded to you for the 1996/97 tax year.

Do you want to calculate your tax?

If you answer 'No' to **Q18**, go to **Q19**.
18.1–18.9 Fill in these boxes only if you are calculating your own tax bill. Get the amounts to put in boxes **18.1** to **18.9** from the working sheets in the tax calculation guide that was sent with your tax return.

Do you want to claim a repayment if you have paid too much tax?

If you answer 'No' to **Q19**, go to **Q20**. If you are not sure at this stage whether you will be due a repayment, you have nothing to lose by ticking the yes box. Otherwise, the Revenue will hang on to any overpayment of tax and set it against future tax bills.

Are your details on the front of the form wrong?

If you answer 'No' to **Q20**, go to **Q21**. If you answer 'Yes', amend the details (name, address, National Insurance number, and so on) as necessary on the front of the form.

Please give other personal details

You don't have to give your telephone number if you don't want to. Put your date of birth only if you claimed relief for pension contributions under **Q14**, or venture capital trust investments under **Q15**, or if you were born before 6 April 1932.

OTHER INFORMATION for the year ended 5 April 1997, continued

Q22 Please tick boxes 22.1 to 22.5 if they apply and provide any additional information in the box below.

Tick box 22.1 if you expect to receive a new pension or Social Security benefit in 1997-98. **22.1**

Tick box 22.2 if you do **not** want any tax you owe collected through your tax code. **22.2**

Tick box 22.3 if this Tax Return contains figures that are provisional because you do not yet have final figures. Give details below. **22.3**

Tick box 22.4 if you have made payments of rent to someone outside the UK. Give their name and address below. **22.4**

Tick box 22.5 if you want to claim:
- relief now for 1997-98 trading losses. Enter the amount and year in the 'Additional information' box below
- to have post-cessation or other business receipts taxed as income of an earlier year. Enter the amount and year in the 'Additional information' box below
- backwards or forwards spreading of literary or artistic income. Enter in the 'Additional information' box details of any amounts spread back to last year and, if appropriate, the year before. **22.5**

Additional information

Q23 **Declaration**

I have filled in and am sending back to you the following pages:

Tick		Tick		Tick
1 TO 8 OF THIS FORM		PARTNERSHIP		TRUSTS ETC
EMPLOYMENT		LAND & PROPERTY		CAPITAL GAINS
SHARE SCHEMES		FOREIGN		NON-RESIDENCE ETC
SELF-EMPLOYMENT				

Before you send your completed Tax Return back to your Tax Office, you must sign the statement below. If you give false information or conceal any part of your income or chargeable gains, you can be prosecuted. You may also have to pay substantial financial penalties.

23.1 The information I have given in this Tax Return is correct and complete to the best of my knowledge and belief.

Signature _____ Date _____

If you have signed for someone else, please also:
- state the capacity in which you are signing (for example, as executor or receiver)

23.2 _____

- give the name of the person you are signing for and **your** name and address in the 'Additional information' box above.

BMSD 12/96 TAX RETURN: PAGE 8

Tax return page 8: Other information continued

YOU WILL NEED to fill in this page to sign and date your tax return. Also, check through boxes **22.1** to **22.5** to see whether any of the miscellaneous items apply to you.

Tick boxes **22.1–22.5** if they apply and provide any additional information in the box below.

22.1 Tick if you expect to start getting a pension or state benefit in the tax year beginning 6 April 1997 or if, by the time you fill in the return, you've already started getting the pension or benefit.

22.2 If you owe tax of less than £1,000, it will normally be collected by a lowering of your tax code under PAYE, if possible. Tick if you don't want the tax collected this way. Before choosing, you may want to check when the tax would otherwise be due. Paying it through PAYE can mean you pay it later than you have to – or sooner, depending on how the tax liability arose.

22.3 Tick if you have included provisional figures anywhere in the tax return and give details in the additional information box. Sending back an incomplete tax return may result in penalties. But your tax inspector may adopt a conciliatory attitude if you send back your return with some provisional figures; explain why they are provisional and say when you expect to give final figures.

22.4 Tick if you are a tenant paying rent to someone outside the UK and put the person's name and address in the additional information box.

22.5 Tick if any of the listed circumstances apply and give details in the additional information box (see explanatory notes).

DECLARATION

Q23 Tick to show that you have filled in pages 2 to 8 of the main tax return and tick the supplementary pages you have filled in.

23.1 Sign and date the return.

23.2 If you have signed this form for someone else, put the capacity in which you are signing. Put the name of the person for whom you are signing and your own name and address in the additional information box.

TAX

11 Working out your income tax bill

As we've said earlier you're not, at present, under any obligation to work out your own tax bill, despite the introduction of self assessment. There may come a time when doing the calculations is compulsory, but for now the Inland Revenue would rather you left it to them.

It's not the easiest thing in the world to do, so unless you are keen on figures and maths, there's no real need to do any calculations. However, there is a real advantage in doing some sums yourself, as you will be able to check that the Inland Revenue gets it right.

If you get a tax return, you will also receive a Tax Calculation Guide which you work through to arrive at the appropriate figure. There are four types of guides:
○ For people who have a capital gains tax bill.
○ For people who receive certain lump sums (from your employer or life insurance).
○ For people who have neither of the above.
○ For people who have both.

The calculations

THE TAX CALCULATION GUIDES that accompany the tax return take you through the calculation, picking up figures from specific boxes on your tax return. If you don't get a tax return, or simply want to see if the Inland Revenue gets the same result as you in working out the bill, you can follow these steps.

The steps involved in working out your tax bill are as follows:
1 Work out your gross income.

2   Deduct any tax-free outgoings.
3   Work out your total income and any tax already paid.
4   Deduct unrestricted allowances.
5   Work out lower-rate tax.
6   Work out basic-rate tax.
7   Work out higher-rate tax.
8   Add up tax.
9   Deduct other reliefs (for example restricted allowances).
10 Deduct tax already paid.

You can use this guide to each step, and the example on page 185, to work out your tax position for 1997/98.

1 WORK OUT YOUR GROSS INCOME

This is simply a question of totting up all the income you have received during the tax year (or the relevant accounting year if you are self-employed). If some of the income you received was paid with the tax already deducted, you will need to add the tax back. Remember, some money you receive is automatically tax free (see Chapter 2). The types of income that you do need to include in your calculations are:

- Income from your job (including the taxable value of your perks), taxable profits from self-employment (see Chapter 5).
- Pension income (see Chapter 7).
- Taxable social security benefits (see Chapter 4).
- Savings and investment income, plus gains from investment-linked life insurance (see Chapter 6).
- Rental income (see Chapter 4).

If you have other types of income and you are not sure where it fits in, check with your tax office.

2 DEDUCT ANY TAX-FREE OUTGOINGS

Some payments that you make can be deducted from your income in order to establish the income you are liable to pay tax on; they include:

- Pension contributions (see Chapter 7).
- Certain maintenance payments (see Chapter 4).
- Donations to charity (see Chapter 2).
- Class 4 National Insurance contributions, made by the self-employed (see Chapter 5).

You need to use the gross amounts of the outgoings.

3 Work out total income
This step simply involves deducting the total from step 2 from the total in step 1.

4 Deduct unrestricted allowances
Chapter 4 runs through all the different allowances to which you may be entitled. Some allowances – the married couple's allowance, for example – cannot be deducted in full here because you get only 15% of the amount of the allowance knocked off your income. These will be deducted in step 9. Deduct the total of your unrestricted allowances from the figure reached in step 3; if your allowances come to more than your income from step 3, you may be entitled to a rebate.

5 Work out lower-rate tax
For the 1997/98 tax year you pay lower-rate tax of 20% on the first £4,100 of your total income – the figure from step 4.
- If your income is less than £4,100, work out 20% of it and go to step 8.
- If your income is more than £4,100, the figure to carry forward is £820 (20% of £4,100). Go to step 6.

6 Work out basic-rate tax
For the 1997/98 tax year you pay basic-rate tax of 23% on your income between £4,100 and £26,100.
- If your total income is over £4,100 but less than £26,100, deduct £4,100 from your total income and work out 23% of the result. Add this to £820 and go to step 8.
- If your total income is over £26,100, the figure to carry forward £5,060. Add this to £820, which gives £5,880. Go to step 7.

7 Work out higher-rate tax
For the 1997/98 tax year you pay higher-rate tax of 40% on your total income over £26,100. Deduct £26,100 from your total income and work out 40% of the result. Add this to £5,880. Go to step 8.

8 Add up total tax
Use the figure you have arrived at for the rest of the calculation.

9 Deduct outstanding allowances and reliefs

There may still be some further reliefs outstanding. These include the restricted allowances (see step 4 and Chapter 4). You can deduct 15% of the relevant allowances from the figure at step 8. You may also be able to deduct amounts for maintenance payments made (see Chapter 4), and for the enterprise investment scheme or venture capital trusts (see Chapter 6).

10 Deduct tax already paid

You can now deduct the amounts of tax you have already paid from the figure arrived at in step 9. So take the tax already paid on income in step 1 and deduct the tax on the outgoings in step 2. Now take the result from the figure arrived at in step 9; this will give you the amount of tax you need to pay. If you get a minus figure, it is the rebate to which you are entitled.

> **Example**
> You are married and have a salary of £35,000, a company car with a taxable value of £3,500, and gross savings interest of £1,200 in the 1997/98 tax year. You made pension contributions of £1,750; this is the gross amount – the tax you would otherwise have paid on them would have been at 40%, which is £700. You have already paid tax of £7,822 through PAYE and £240 tax has been deducted from your savings interest. You work out the tax now due as follows:
> 1. Add up your salary, the taxable value of the car, and the savings interest to get £39,700.
> 2. Your outgoings consist of the pension contributions of £1,750.
> 3. Deduct £1,750 from £39,700 to get £37,950.
> 4. Deduct the personal allowance of £4,045 for the 1997/98 tax year from £37,950 to get £33,905.
> 5. Income is more than £4,100, so carry forward £820.
> 6. Income is more than £26,100, so carry forward £5,880.
> 7. Deduct £26,100 from £33,905, which gives £7,805. 40% of £7,805 is £3,122.
> 8. Add £5,880 and £3,122 to get £9,002.
> 9. Deduct £274.50 (15% of married couple's allowance of £1,830 for the 1997/98 tax year) from £9,002, which is £8,727.50.
> 10. You can now deduct the tax you have already paid, so add £7,822 to £240 and deduct £700 (the 40% tax on your pension contributions); this gives £7,362. Taking this from £8,727.50 means there is tax of £1,365.50 still to pay.

Inland Revenue calculations

If you receive a tax calculation from the Inland Revenue, you'll find that it looks slightly different to the final steps described above. The Revenue works it out by building up the rate in stages.

1. You pay at least 20% tax on all your taxable income, so it works out 20% of your taxable income.
2. You pay at least the basic rate of tax – 23% for 1997/98 – on the rest of your taxable income. So the Inland Revenue deducts the lower rate band – £4,100 from your taxable income. It's already worked out 20% of this so it just needs to work out the balance – 3%.
3. If your taxable income is over the limit for higher-rate tax, which is £26,000 for 1997/98, it deducts £26,100 from your taxable income. Having already taken account of 23% of this amount in steps 1 and 2, it works out 17% of this amount to mean you'll pay 40% tax on it.

So, in the example on page 184, the bill would be worked out as follows:

	£
£33,905 at 20%	6,781.00
£29,805 (£33,905 less £4,100) @ 3%	894.15
£7,805 (£33,905 less £26,100) @ 17%	1,326.85
	9,002.00

Bear in mind when you receive a tax calculation for the 1996/97 tax year, the basic rate of tax for that year was 24% (the other rates were the same) and the tax bands were:

Lower rate – first £3,900 of taxable income
Basic rate – up to £25,500
Higher rate – over £25,500.

Help!

IF YOU HAVE ACCESS to a computer, you might find it is worth investing in one of the software packages which do this task for you. Most cost around £50. You enter the figures as you would on your tax return and the computer does the sums for you.

There is also an electronic version of the tax return. You can get hold of a disk by calling the Inland Revenue Orderline on 0645 000404.

TAX

12 Complaints and tax return enquiries

So far in this book, we've explained how things should work. Unfortunately, the complexity of the tax system can mean that things don't always run smoothly, but there are clear procedures and guidelines for what should happen if you run into difficulties with the Revenue.

Your tax return plays a significant part in your communication with the Inland Revenue. Once your form has been received the Revenue may decide to make further enquiries into the information you've supplied. This chapter explains the process involved in sorting out problems and tax return enquiries.

APPEALS

One of the consequences of self assessment should be that you do not need to appeal against an assessment – you have supplied the information, and so long as you pay your tax on time there should not be any problems. You cannot appeal against an Inland Revenue enquiry (see page 190), but you can appeal against surcharges and penalties, requests for documents during an enquiry, or the way an enquiry is handled, or an Inland Revenue amendment to your assessment. You obviously need to be able to justify your appeal.

You appeal first to your tax inspector. If this fails you can then make an appeal to the general commissioners or the special commissioners. General commissioners are laypeople who are advised by an expert clerk, and they deal with most cases. Special Commissioners are tax experts and they deal with cases that require an understanding of tax law. If a point of law is in dispute, it is possible that your case may go to the Court of Appeal and possibly the House of Lords. But your case should be solved by the commissioners.

COMPLAINTS

If you are unhappy with the way the Inland Revenue has handled your affairs, you should write to the person in charge of the relevant office or unit – his or her name should be on any correspondence you have had from that office.

If the matter is not resolved to your satisfaction you should then write to the Controller for the area – you can get the right name and address from any tax office.

If the Controller is unable to settle your complaint, the next step is to write to the Inland Revenue Adjudicator, currently Elizabeth Filkin. The address is on page 210. The Adjudicator is an impartial referee who will look into any complaint about problems arising since 5 April 1993. The types of complaint the Adjudicator can review include excessive delay, errors, discourtesy and the way in which the Inland Revenue has – or has not – exercised discretion.

You should complain to the Adjudicator as soon as possible after you have been unable to settle the problem with the Inland Revenue. He or she will not normally look at your complaint if you write more than six months after the relevant Controller has provided an answer with which you are dissatisfied. Your letter to the Adjudicator should include your name and address, it should explain exactly what you're dissatisfied with, and give the name of the relevant tax office and your tax reference number (you should find this on any correspondence from your tax office). You should state clearly what it is that you want from the Inland Revenue to settle your complaint, and detail any costs incurred as a result of the subject of your complaint. If you're happy for the adjudicator to contact you by telephone, include a daytime number.

The Adjudicator will then decide whether your case can be looked at. If it can't be looked at, you will be informed why. If it does come within the Adjudicator's remit, the Inland Revenue will be asked for a full report of its side of the story, and you

> Tax expert and *Moneywise* Ask the Professionals panellist Janet Adam says:
>
> "The Adjudicator is there to reach an impartial decision as to how particular matters may have been handled by the Inland Revenue. She is not concerned with agreeing how much tax is actually payable but just to decide whether matters have been dealt with properly and efficiently by the Inland Revenue in the light of information available to it."

may be asked for more information. Once there is a full picture of events, the Adjudicator will see if there is any scope for you and the Inland Revenue to come to an agreement and contact you both with suggestions.

If the Adjudicator does not think this is possible, or you still don't reach an agreement with the Inland Revenue, the Adjudicator will make a formal recommendation to the Inland Revenue about how your complaint should be settled. This will also be sent to you.

Your complaint may be upheld wholly or in part – or the Adjudicator may decide that the Inland Revenue has been reasonable and reject your complaint. In 1996, 2,028 cases were clarified and referred back to the Inland Revenue's complaints procedure; 495 full investigations were completed, with 28 complaints withdrawn, 228 not upheld, and 239 upheld. Compensation was paid in 86 cases. The main complaints were about mistakes, delays, and the way the Inland Revenue may or may not have exercised discretion.

The Inland Revenue will then act upon the Adjudicator's recommendations in all but 'exceptional circumstances'. If it doesn't act upon them, this will have to be explained to the Adjudicator and will be included in his or her annual report, without naming the taxpayer involved.

There is a code of practice setting out the circumstances in which – if it is responsible for long delays or a serious mistake – the Inland Revenue will pay interest on late repayments of tax to you, not collect tax or interest on tax that is strictly due, and pay costs incurred as a result of the delay or mistake. The Adjudicator may decide that the code of practice applies in your case and refer to it in his or her recommendation. The Inland Revenue will also make exceptional consolatory payments for worry and distress caused.

The Adjudicator tries to settle complaints as quickly as possible. In 1996, on average, the Adjudicator completed investigations in just over four-and-a-half months. In the 1997 annual report, the current Adjudicator explains that she believes the Inland Revenue is improving but still has problems.

You can also write to your MP, who may take up your case with the Inland Revenue or the Treasury. Or you can ask your MP to refer your case to the Parliamentary Ombudsman (formally known as Parliamentary Commissioner for Administration).

> **Summary box – Adjudicator**
>
> 1. The Adjudicator decides whether or not to deal with your case. If not, you will be informed why. The Adjudicator then gets the Inland Revenue's version of events.
>
> 2. If possible, the Adjudicator will make suggestions to you and to the Inland Revenue to help resolve the matter.
>
> 3. If this is not possible or does not work, the Adjudicator makes a formal recommendation to the Inland Revenue.
>
> 4. If, after all that, you are still unhappy, you can then ask your MP to refer your case to the Parliamentary Ombudsman.

ENQUIRIES INTO TAX RETURNS

The Inland Revenue may decide to make enquiries into your tax return. It can do so up to 12 months after the return was due in – longer if you sent it back late. According to the Inland Revenue this is for two reasons: first it wants you to pay the correct amount of tax; second it wants you to feel confident that other taxpayers are paying what they should and that the system is operated fairly.

When the Inland Revenue receives your tax return it uses your figures to establish the tax you should pay, or that should be repaid to you. If there are obvious mistakes it may correct them without making further enquiries, and you will be sent details of the corrected figures. If you disagree with what has been done you can discuss this with the Inland Revenue, and if appropriate, the figures can be amended again.

The Inland Revenue checks the information you have supplied with information from other sources. For example from your bank or building society, or companies for which you've done work on a self-employed basis. Once these checks have been carried out, the Inland Revenue may start enquiries if it believes your return is incorrect, or requires fuller explanation. It will also look further into some tax returns at random. It will be your tax office which carries out the enquiries.

> Tax expert and *Moneywise* Ask the Professionals panellist Janet Adam says:
>
> "Under self assessment the Inland Revenue has random powers of enquiry. A list of taxpayers is chosen at random centrally, prior to the issue of tax returns. In addition to this, tax offices will enquire into other returns where they believe inconsistencies arise. You will not be entitled to know whether or not you have been chosen at random."

The Inland Revenue will tell you in writing if it intends to start enquiries and should give details of the information it requires. This may be limited to one or two aspects of the return, e.g. further clarification of entries, or checking original records. It may decide to examine all your tax affairs in detail, which would entail a thorough review of the records on which your return was based.

The Inland Revenue aims to take up as little of your time as possible, and will avoid asking for information in a piecemeal fashion where possible. Its code of practice on enquiries allows a reasonable amount of time to provide information, and if you don't think it's enough you should explain why. Extra time will be granted for reasonable cases.

This also applies if you have difficulty getting hold of the information needed – the Inland Revenue should be able to make suggestions as to how you can obtain it. If you do not provide the information asked for, there may be penalties to pay.

If you are in business, the Inland Revenue can examine your records at your place of work if it happens to be more convenient. The Inland Revenue will also return your records as soon as possible; in the meantime you can ask for the return of specific items. It is prepared to send them back to you as long as you can give an idea of when you'll return them. If it needs them it will give you copies.

If you believe you've provided all the information and explanations the Inland Revenue should need, but enquiries are still going on, you can ask why. If you think there are no grounds for the enquiries to continue you can ask the Appeal Commissioners to decide whether the enquiry should be closed. The Inland Revenue may ask to meet you, and if you have a professional adviser, he or she can attend the meeting. You don't have to go to any meeting, but it might give you the best opportunity to explain anything that might have been misunderstood. It's obviously best to be honest and if you don't know the answer to something you should say so. If you realise after the meeting that something you said was wrong you should let the Inland Revenue know. Its officers will make notes of any meeting and you are entitled to a copy. You may be asked to sign the notes, indicating they are correct.

Once it is satisfied the Inland Revenue will confirm to you that there is nothing wrong and the enquiries have finished; if there is something wrong it will try to agree any revised figures with you, and explain how it has arrived at the new figures – you should ask for an explanation if you don't understand this. If you agree with the new figures you have 30 days to amend your tax return. If you disagree you have 30 days to appeal to independent Appeal Commissioners. The Inland Revenue will try to reach agreement with you, without the need for a formal appeal.

You may be asked to make a payment on account towards any additional tax the Inland Revenue believes may be due. You don't have to pay it, but remember you may have to pay interest on top of any extra tax the Revenue finds you owe. If you've paid some or all of it already you'll pay less or no interest. If it turns out that you've paid too much, the money will be repaid with interest.

PENALTIES

- If you miss the final deadline for sending back your tax return (31 January 1998) you'll have to pay a fixed penalty of £100.
- If you still haven't sent it back six months later you'll charged another £100. In serious cases the Inland Revenue may start charging £60 a day.
- If you are late paying tax you will be charged interest (at 9.5%). There will be a 5% surcharge as well if the tax isn't paid by 28 February. If you still haven't paid the tax by 31 July the surcharge goes up to 10%.

If you have a reasonable excuse for missing deadlines, you may be able to appeal against the penalties. It is also important to keep records as you can be fined up to £3,000 for each failure to keep records in support of information supplied on the tax return. The maximum would be charged only where someone had wilfully destroyed records to hide information, otherwise each case would be dealt with individually.

MISTAKES

If the Inland Revenue makes a serious mistake in dealing with your tax affairs it will pay any reasonable costs you incur as a direct result, such as postage or telephone charges, lost earnings, or professional fees. It also pays these if it persistently makes less serious errors. If you pay too much tax because of a mistake by the Inland

Summary box – enquiries

1. The Inland Revenue informs you in writing that it intends to start enquiries, and gives you details of the information it requires.

2. The Inland Revenue may wish to review the records upon which your return is based. If you are self-employed this could be done at your place of business. Otherwise you need to supply the records to your tax office, which should return them to you as soon as possible.

3. The Inland Revenue may ask to meet face to face. It makes notes of meetings. You are entitled to a copy.

4. If it considers there is something wrong, the Inland Revenue will try to agree any revised figures with you.

5. If you agree with the new figures you have 30 days to amend your return.

6. If you disagree, appeal to the Appeal Commissioners within 30 days.

Revenue, you can claim a repayment for any affected year going back 20 years. If you pay too much tax because of an error you make on your tax return, you can claim repayment up to six years later. If you don't pay enough because of a mistake you behalf, you'll have to pay interest on the tax that is paid late.

Action plan

- If you have a problem with the Inland Revenue you should complain first to your tax office, and if it is not resolved to the Regional Controller and then the Adjudicator.

- Be clear about what has gone wrong and what you want to happen when you make a complaint.

- Make any complaint as soon as possible after any problem arises

- If the Inland Revenue decides to make enquiries into your tax return, don't be alarmed, and provide any documents it requires.

- If you're asked to pay additional tax while the bill is being finalised it's best to pay it even if it turns out not to be due. The Inland Revenue will have to pay you back with interest.

- If you think your tax office is in error, let it know as soon as possible. If you've made a mistake on your tax return, the same applies.

TAX

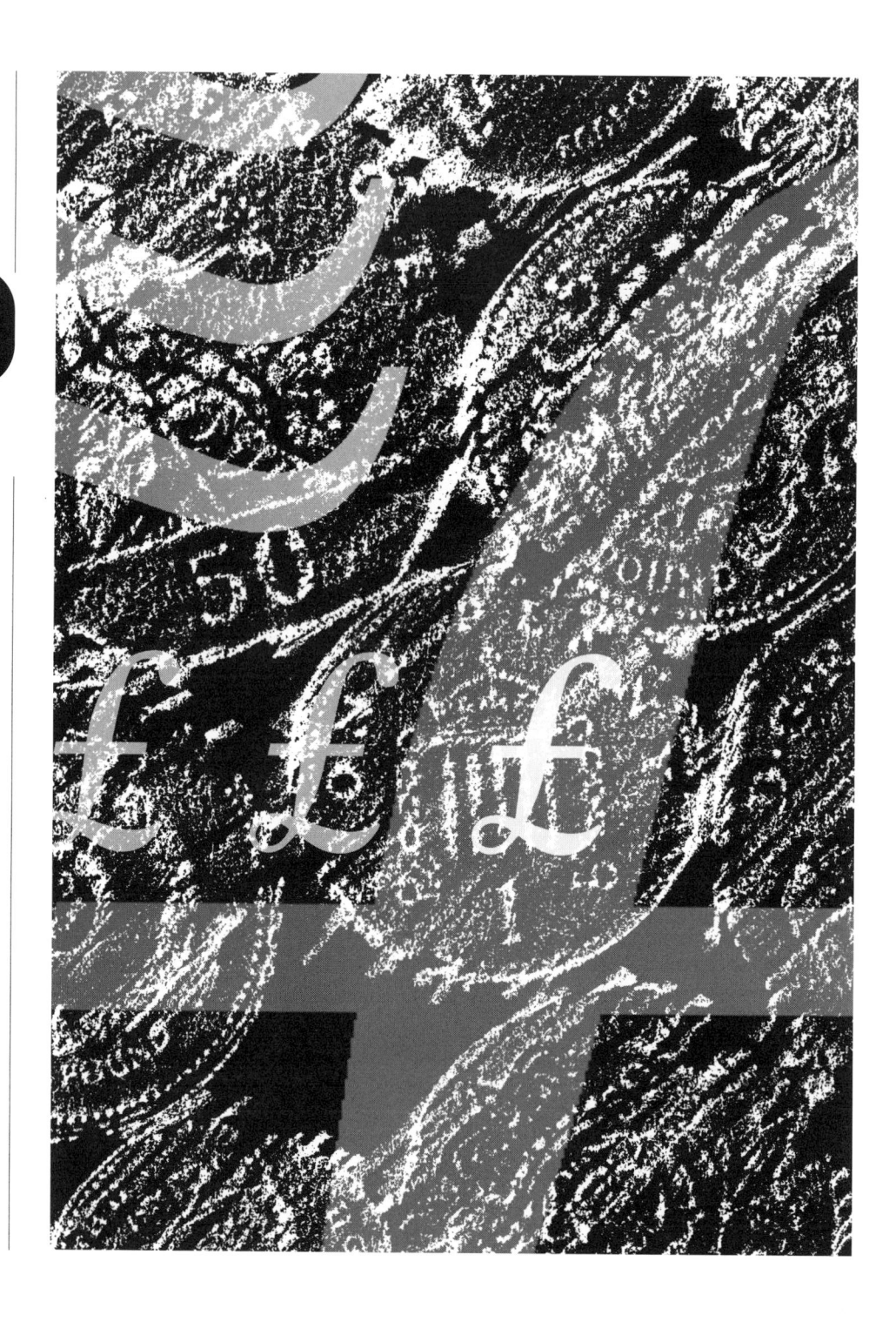

Inland Revenue leaflets

This chapter contains a comprehensive list of all Inland Revenue leaflets currently available.

Personal taxpayer series

INCOME TAX

IR33 Income tax and school leavers
A basic guide aimed at young people. It explains what income tax, PAYE, tax allowances and tax codes are. It also forms part of an education resource pack *Tax for you*, which is aimed at young people, especially those who are just about to leave school.

IR34 Pay as you earn
This is aimed at all employees who want to know more about the PAYE system.

IR41 Income tax and job seekers
Jobseeker's Allowance (JSA) replaced Unemployment Benefit and Income Support for unemployed people in October 1996. This leaflet is for people who are claiming JSA because they do not have a job. It explains how tax is affected by unemployment and whether or not you can claim a tax refund when you are unemployed.

IR42 Lay-off and short-time work
This is a guide for people who have a job but are claiming benefits because they have been laid-off or are on short-time work.

IR43 Income tax and strikes
A basic guide for people who have a job but are claiming because they are on strike.

IR58 Going to work abroad?
This leaflet answers many of the questions about tax where a UK resident works abroad as an employee.

IR60 Income tax and students
If you are a student this leaflet will help you understand the income tax system and how it affects you. It explains tax allowances, holiday earnings, and unemployment benefit.

IR68 Accrued income scheme: Taxing securities on transfer
The accrued income scheme changes the way income tax is charged when certain securities are transferred from one person to another. This leaflet explains the basic rules of the scheme as they apply to individuals.

IR80 Income tax and married couples
This leaflet outlines the allowances and reliefs that can be claimed by married couples who are living together.

IR90 Tax allowances and reliefs
This describes the main allowances and reliefs that are available to set against income tax and how to claim them.

IR91 A guide for widows and widowers
This explains how income tax affects widows and widowers. It is intended to help those who have been bereaved recently.

IR92 A guide for one-parent families
This leaflet tells you what kinds of income are taxed and what tax allowances you may be able to claim as a one-parent family.

IR93 Separation, divorce and maintenance payments
This leaflet answers the sorts of questions people ask about tax when they separate or divorce. It tells you about legally enforceable maintenance payments which receive tax relief, and voluntary payments which do not.

IR121 Income tax and pensioners
This leaflet tells you about personal allowances, how these can be affected by income and what kinds of income are taxable and

what are not. It is particularly helpful if you are just about to become a pensioner.

IR122 Volunteer drivers
This leaflet is for volunteers who drive for a charity, voluntary organisation, or local authority. It tells you how to work out whether tax is due on any mileage or other allowances you receive towards the cost of running your car.

IR125 Using your own car for work
This booklet is for employees who use their own cars for business journeys. It tells you how using your own car for work affects your tax, how car or mileage allowances are taxed, how to work out your business motoring costs, and what information you should give to the Inland Revenue.

IR133 Income tax and company cars from 6 April 1994: A guide for employees
If your employer provides you with a car that you can use for private travel it is a benefit in kind and you may have to pay tax on it. This booklet explains how the system works.

IR134 Income tax and relocation packages
If your employer helps you to move house, any payments you receive, or any goods or services provided for you are part of your taxable earnings. This leaflet explains how you are taxed if you receive this type of help.

IR136 Income tax and company vans: A guide for employees and employers
How the private use of a company van is taxed. This leaflet answers the questions most often asked by both employees and employers.

IR144 Income tax and incapacity benefit
This leaflet is for people who are claiming Incapacity Benefit. It explains how it is taxed and how you can get help from the tax office if you need it.

EMPLOYEE SHARE SCHEMES

IR16 Share acquisitions by directors and employees: Explanatory notes
This booklet describes the circumstances in which income tax may become chargeable to directors and employees on the grant and exercise of options to acquire shares. It also covers the acquisition of shares generally.

IR17 Share acquisitions by directors and employees: An outline for employees
This leaflet tells you about the income tax you may have to pay on any shares or share options you get because of your job. This applies whether you are a director or an employee.

IR95 Approved profit sharing schemes: An outline for employees
You may be able to share in the profits of the company you work for in a number of ways. This booklet gives brief details of the tax relief available.

IR97 Approved Save As You Earn share option schemes: An outline for employees
This booklet describes the tax advantages if you join a savings-related share option scheme that has been set up by the company you work for.

IR101 Approved company share option plans: An outline for employees
This booklet explains briefly about the tax advantages available to you if your company sets up a share option plan which is approved by the Inland Revenue.

SAVINGS AND INVESTMENTS

IR78 Personal pensions: A guide for tax
This describes what personal pensions are about, how they work, who can provide them, the tax reliefs available, how to make an investment, the tax advantages, how much you can pay in, and what plan managers do – essentially, it is a basic guide to a fairly complex subject.

IR89 Personal Equity Plans (PEPs): A guide for potential investors
This leaflet describes the two types of PEPs that are available, how to make an investment, the tax advantages, how much you can pay in, and what plan managers do – again, it is a basic guide to a fairly complex subject.

IR103 Tax relief for private medical insurance: For people aged 60 or over
This leaflet explains how you can get tax relief for premiums paid under a private medical insurance contract if you are 60 years of age or older.

IR110 A guide for people with savings
Do you have to pay tax on your savings? Banks, building societies and local authorities are all required by law to take income tax off the interest they pay to savers. However, people whose taxable income is covered by their tax allowances can register to get their interest gross (that is, without having the tax taken off). This guide explains how to work out whether or not you can claim tax back and how to register in order to ensure you get your interest gross.

IR114 TESSAs: Tax-free interest for taxpayers
A guide that explains the rules for tax-exempt special savings accounts. You can open a TESSA if you are a taxpayer but want to receive tax-free interest. New rules mean you can open a follow-up TESSA when your first TESSA has matured after five years.

IR129 Occupational pension schemes: An introduction
This leaflet will help you if you are thinking about joining an employers pension scheme.

CAPITAL GAINS TAX

CGT4 Capital gains tax: Owner-occupied houses
This leaflet answers the most common questions about CGT and owner-occupied housing. It also describes the rules that may affect you if you rent out part of your home or use part of it for business purposes.

CGT14 Capital gains tax: An introduction
This leaflet sets out the basic rules of CGT for individuals: it explains what a disposal is, what kind of assets CGT applies to, and includes some examples showing you how to calculate gains and losses.

CGT16 Capital gains tax: Indexation allowance – Disposals after 5 April 1988
This shows you how the indexation allowance applies to assets. The allowance is an adjustment for inflation when calculating gains. It increases the cost of the asset in line with the RPI.

GENERAL

IR37 Appeals against tax
This leaflet explains the procedure for making a tax appeal. It is intended mainly for people who do not have professional advice in dealing with their tax affairs.

IR45 What to do when someone dies
This leaflet will help you understand the tax consequences that arise when someone dies. It gives information about income tax, capital gains tax, and inheritance tax. There are sections about the responsibilities of personal representatives and trustees, and about the tax treatment of beneficiaries.

IR65 Giving to charity: How individuals can get tax relief
A brief explanation of how you can get tax relief on gifts made to UK charities through the payroll giving scheme, deeds of covenant, and Gift Aid.

IR87 Letting and your home: Including the rent-a-room scheme and letting your previous home when you live elsewhere
This leaflet shows how income from letting furnished rooms is treated for tax purposes. It explains the expenses you are allowed to claim, capital allowances and capital gains tax. It also explains the rules of the rent-a-room scheme, which allows you to let furnished accommodation in your home without having to pay tax on the rent you receive, so long as the income derived does not exceed £4,250 in 1997/98.

IR115 Tax and childcare
This leaflet explains the tax and National Insurance rules relating to childcare. It also gives parents and employers other useful information about their tax position.

IR119 Tax relief for vocational training
Are you training for a National Vocational Qualification (NVQ) or a Scottish Vocational Qualification (SVQ), up to and including Level 4? This leaflet shows you how tax relief is available on the payments you make for the training.

IR120 You and the Inland Revenue: Tax, Collection and Accounts Offices
Are you happy with the service you have received from the Inland Revenue? Do you have any comments or suggestions for improvement? This leaflet tells you how to get help and information, and includes the Taxpayer's Charter, which sets out the standard of service you can expect from the Inland Revenue. The leaflet is available in versions for the Pension Schemes Office, Capital Taxes Office, Financial Intermediaries and Claims Office, Special Compliance Office, and Enforcement Office.

IR123 Mortgage interest relief: Buying your home
A short guide to mortgage interest relief for a loan to buy your home. It explains which loans qualify for mortgage interest relief at source (MIRAS), how the relief is given to you, and how it is shared out if you are buying with someone else.

IR141 Open Government
In April 1994 the government introduced the 'Code of Practice on Access to Government Information'. This leaflet explains how the Inland Revenue is complying with the code.

IR152 Trusts: An introduction
This leaflet is a short guide to trusts and how they are taxed. It covers the basic types of private family trusts, but not special trusts or non-resident trusts.

IR156 Our heritage: Your right to see tax-exempt works of art
Privately owned works of art and other objects which are broadly

part of our national heritage can be exempted from taxes on capital such as inheritance tax. You have a right to see these exempt works of art and other objects. This leaflet tells you more about that right, what you can see, and how.

SELF ASSESSMENT SERIES

SA/BK1 Self Assessment: A general guide
This is a guide to a new way of working out tax if you get a tax return. It tells you what is new and how it affects you.

SA/BK2 Self Assessment: A guide for the self-employed
This guide tells you how tax for self-employed people is worked out. It tells you what is new and how it affects you.

SA/BK3 Self Assessment: A guide to keeping records for the self-employed
Until recently there was no legal requirement to keep records for income tax, but rules introduced in the 1994 Finance Act mean that you now have to keep all appropriate records. This guide gives general advice about what business records you need to keep for tax purposes each tax year, and how long you need to hold on to them.

SA/BK4 Self Assessment: A general guide to keeping records
Everyone who pays tax should receive a record of the tax they have paid. The law now requires that you keep these and other records so that you can complete a tax return fully and accurately if you are asked to do so. These records may also be needed if you need to make a claim, for example, for tax allowances. This guide gives advice on the records you need to keep.

Business series

GENERAL

CWL1 Starting your own business?
This booklet is the first in a series which will be produced jointly

by the Inland Revenue, HM Customs and Excise, and the Contributions Agency, which are working together to provide a better service to businesses. It is for anyone setting up in business and deals with income tax, VAT, and National Insurance contributions. The leaflet tells you what you need to tell the Inland Revenue and how to get things right from the start. It contains a form that you can use to notify all three departments when you start your business.

IR56/N139 Employed or self-employed? A guide for tax and National Insurance This can help you decide – if you are in any doubt –whether or not you are employed or self-employed, an area that frequently causes a lot of confusion. It also tells you how tax and National Insurance affect you, whatever your employment status.

IR137 The Enterprise Investment Scheme
The EIS has been set up by the government to assist certain types of unquoted companies to raise finance from outside investors. This booklet provides a general outline of how the scheme works, and who is eligible.

480 Expenses and benefits: A guide for tax
This tells you which expenses payments and benefits are taxable and which are not. It describes, among other things, dispensations, the use of cars, and entertaining expenses.

Capital gains tax

CGT6 Retirement relief on disposal of a business: Capital gains tax
If you are 55 or older and are in the process of disposing of a business, or some other type of asset such as shares in your family company, this leaflet should be helpful. It also provides some practical examples.

Self-employed people

IR24 Class 4 National Insurance contributions
Self-employed people pay Class 4 contributions on profits from

any trade, profession or vocation. This leaflet explains how income is affected by these contributions and what tax relief is available.

IR105 How your profits are taxed
This leaflet you about assessments of tax and accounting years. It also describes how to work out your business profits especially in the early years of trading. There is also some helpful advice if you find yourself in the position where you have to wind down a business.

Capital Taxes Office series

IHT3 Inheritance tax: An introduction
Some basic facts about IHT. You should find it useful if you want to know whether or not tax will have to be paid on your estate after your death.

International series

IR20 Residents and non-residents: Liability to tax in the United Kingdom
This booklet describes the residence rules relating to tax and how to work out whether or not you are resident in the UK for tax purposes.

IR138 Living or retiring abroad? A guide to UK tax on your UK income and pension
This booklet explains how the income from your investments in the UK and your UK pension will be taxed if you decide to live or retire abroad.

IR139 Income from abroad? A guide to UK tax on overseas income
This booklet explains how overseas income is taxed in the UK and how you can obtain relief from double taxation if your overseas income is subject to tax both in the UK and in another country.

Clubs and charities series

IR75 Tax reliefs for charities

Charities benefit from important tax reliefs. This booklet describes how they can qualify and explains tax exemptions and charitable expenditure.

IR113 Gift Aid: A guide for donors and charities
Gift Aid is tax relief for single cash gifts to charity. This booklet explains how individuals and companies can use the scheme.

Codes of Practice

Code of Practice 1: Mistakes by the Inland Revenue
There are occasions when the Inland Revenue makes mistakes. This booklet sets out how a taxpayer may claim some redress when, for instance, the Inland Revenue causes delay or persists in getting something wrong.

Code of Practice 2: Investigations
If your affairs are being investigated, you still have the same rights as any other taxpayer. This booklet tells you how local tax offices carry out an investigation. It promises that you will be treated fairly and courteously, in accordance with the law and the Taxpayer's Charter.

The Adjudicator's Office

AO1 How to complain about the Inland Revenue
This leaflet explains how you can complain to the Adjudicator if you are unhappy about the way the Inland Revenue has dealt with your tax affairs. The Adjudicator, whose services are free, acts as an impartial referee who hears both sides of a complaint and who makes recommendations about putting matters right if the complaint is justified.

An A–Z guide to financial words and phrases

Accrual rate The rate at which pension entitlement builds up. Often expressed as a fraction of your final salary for each year served, for example 1/60, 1/80. Can be used to refer to Inland Revenue limits on how a pension entitlement builds up. Also can refer to the actual pension entitlement built up for each year of membership of a final salary company pension scheme.

Additional voluntary contributions (AVCs) Extra payments paid into company pension schemes by members to improve their benefits.

Annual percentage rate (APR) The real cost, in terms of interest and fees, of credit (used for comparison purposes).

Annuity A form of income bought through insurance companies with the proceeds from a pension fund, which pays a guaranteed sum throughout your lifetime.

Base rate The interest rate set by the Bank of England, used as a basis for the rates that banks offer their customers.

Basic state pension Flat rate pension payable to all individuals who have made sufficient National Insurance contributions.

Bid-to-offer spread The difference between the price at which investments can be bought and the price at which they can then be sold.

Bond A certificate of debt issued by companies and governments to raise cash, usually paying interest and traded in a market.

Capital gains tax (CGT) The tax payable on profits from the sale of assets, particularly shares.

Contracting out A legal arrangement under which you can give up part of your SERPS benefits and build up an equivalent or better benefit in a company scheme or personal pension.

Convertible A security, usually a bond or debenture issued by a company, that can be converted into the ordinary shares or preference shares of that company at a fixed date or dates, and at a fixed price.

Deed of covenant A promise made in a deed, often used as a means of providing funds to charities or to transfer income from one person to another, with a view to saving tax.

Derivative A financial instrument that is valued according to the expected price movements of an underlying asset, for example a share or a currency.

Dividend The distribution of part of the earnings of a company to its shareholders

Earnings per share (EPS) The earnings of a company over a stated period, usually a year, divided by the number of ordinary shares it has issued.

Endowment policy A life insurance and savings policy which pays a specified amount of money on an agreed date, or on the death of the person insured, whichever is sooner.

Equities The ordinary shares of a publicly quoted company.

European Currency Unit (ECU) A form of currency calculated as a weighted average of a basket of EC currencies.

Final salary pension scheme a Company pension scheme in which your pension depends on your salary at retirement, your number of years' service, and the fraction of final salary awarded for each year's service, for example 1/60.

Free-standing additional voluntary contributions (FSAVCs) Extra payments made to boost a pension by investing with an insurance company, not an employers scheme. See 'AVCs'.
Friendly Society A mutual organisation offering tax-free investment plans with a life-insurance element, normally over ten years.
Fund A reserve of money or investments held for a specific purpose – for example, to be divided into units for investors to buy (as in a unit trust fund) or to provide a pension income (as in a pension fund).
Future A contract to buy or sell a fixed number of commodities, currencies, or shares at a fixed date in the future at a fixed price.
Gearing The ratio of the amount of long-term loans and preference shares to ordinary shares in a company.
Gilt-edged security (gilt) A fixed-interest security issued by the British Government.
Guaranteed income bond (GIB) A bond guaranteeing the full return of capital plus a fixed income, issued by life insurance companies.
Held in trust An arrangement allowing property or cash to be held by a trustee on behalf of a named beneficiary.
Independent financial adviser (IFA) An adviser committed to offering 'best advice' on the range of investments and plans in the marketplace, not someone selling investments from just one company.

Inheritance tax (IHT) A form of wealth tax on inherited money: £215,000 can be inherited before this tax is incurred.
Initial charge The charge paid to the managers of a unit trust by an investor when he or she first buys units – usually between 3% and 5%.
Investment trust A company quoted on the stock exchange which invests in other companies' shares.
Lower earnings limit (LEL) Weekly wage roughly equivalent to the basic state pension. If you earn less than this amount, you do not pay National Insurance contributions. If you earn more that the LEL, your earnings up to the upper earnings limit (UEL) are liable to National Insurance contributions. Earnings between the LEL and the UEL are called middle band earnings.
Middle band earnings Earnings between the lower and upper earnings limits. The SERPS pension relates to these earnings.
Money purchase pension scheme A company pension scheme in which your pension is dependent on the amount paid into the pension fund, and the investment performance of that fund.
Mortgage interest relief at source (MIRAS) Tax relief at 15% (10% from April 1998) on the interest on the first £30,000 borrowed to buy a house.
National Insurance contributions Contributions payable on earnings if you earn more than the lower earnings limit, to pay for state benefits and pensions.
Negative equity The condition whereby the current market value of a house is worth less than the amount outstanding on a mortgage.
Net relevant earnings Earnings from self-employment or employment which are used to calculate the maximum payments into a personal pension.
Nominees Individuals or companies which hold shares on behalf of investors, to reduce the costs of administering a portfolio, or to conceal the true owners of the shares.
Offshore funds Funds based outside the UK for tax reasons.
Open market option The right to use a pension fund on retirement to buy an annuity from any insurance company, not just the provider of the pension plan.
Option A contract giving the right (but not the obligation) to buy or sell commodities, currencies or shares at a fixed date in the future at a fixed price.
Pay as you earn (PAYE) The system whereby employers collect tax from employees and pass it on to the Inland Revenue.
Penny shares Securities with a very low market price – investors usually hope for rapid recoveries or takeovers.
Pensionable earnings Earnings on which pension benefits and/or contributions are calculated.

Pensionable service The length of time in a particular job which qualifies for pension benefit. Usually this equates to the length of time as a member of the pension scheme.

Pension transfer A payment made from one pension scheme to another, or to an insurance company running a personal pension scheme to fund a buy-out scheme. Enables pension rights to be moved out of the pension scheme of a previous employer.

Permanent health insurance (PHI) Insurance which replaces income lost due to long-term illness or injury and pays benefits relative to the size of a salary.

Personal allowances Amounts of income which you are allowed tax free.

Personal equity plan (PEP) A plan used to hold UK shares, unit trusts, investment trusts, and now corporate bonds, with any dividends and capital gains free of tax.

Personal pension plan An approved scheme for people who are self-employed or not in a company scheme. Personal pensions are arranged through insurance companies, and are individual money purchase schemes.

Preserved pensions Pension rights built up in a pension scheme, which have been left in that scheme when you ceased employment with that company.

Price/earnings ratio (P/E ratio) The market price of a company share divided by the earnings per share of that company.

Retail price index (RPI) The official measure of inflation calculated by weighting the costs of goods and services to approximate a typical family spending pattern.

Retirement annuity contract A type of personal pension superseded in 1988 by personal pensions themselves.

Rights issue New shares sold by a company to raise new capital.

Scrip issue The issue of new share certificates to existing shareholders to reflect an accumulation of profits on the balance sheet.

Self-invested personal pension (SIPP) A personal pension under which the member has the ability to control the investments.

Share An investment in and part ownership of a company, conferring the right to part of the company's profits (usually by payment of a dividend), and to any voting rights attached to that share, and which, in the case of public companies, can be traded on the open market.

Split-capital investment trust A limited-life investment trust in which the equity capital is divided into income shares and capital shares.

State earnings-related pension scheme (SERPS) A state pension in addition to the basic state pension, plus widows' benefits and invalidity benefits, based on earnings.

Stockmarket A market for the buying and selling of shares and securities.

Tax-exempt special savings accounts (TESSAs) Five-year savings accounts which are exempt from tax, and available from banks and building societies.

Tax year The tax system works on the basis of tax years which run from 6 April one calendar year to 5 April the next.

Term assurance or insurance Life insurance with no investment element.

Unit-linked policy An insurance policy in which the benefits depend on the performance of units in a fund invested in shares or property.

Unit trust A pooled fund of stockmarket investments divided into equal units.

Upper earnings limit The maximum weekly wage above which there is no liability to National Insurance contributions.

Value-added tax (VAT) A form of indirect taxation borne by traders and consumers, levied on goods and services.

Whole-of-life policy A life insurance policy which pays a specified amount on the death of the life insured.

With-profits policy A life insurance or pension policy with additional amounts added to the sum insured.

Yield The income from an investment.

Zero-rated Goods or services that are liable to VAT, but with a tax rate of zero.

Directory

REGULATORY BODIES

Investment Managers Regulatory Organisation (IMRO)
Lloyds Chambers, 1 Portsoken Street, London E1 8BT
0171 390 5000

Investors' Compensation Scheme (ICS)
Gavrelle House, 2–14 Bunhill Row, London EC1Y 8RA
0171 638 1240

The Office of the Investment Ombudsman
6 Frederick's Place, London EC2R 8BT
0171 769 3065

Personal Investment Authority (PIA)
1 Canada Square, Canary Wharf, London E14 5AZ
0171 538 8860

Securities and Futures Authority Ltd (SFA)
Cotton Centre, Cottons Lane, London SE1 2QB
0171 378 9000

Securities and Investments Board (SIB)
Gavrelle House, 2–14 Bunhill Row, London EC1Y 8RA
0171 638 1240
SIB Central Register (address as above) 0171 929 3652

SAVINGS AND INVESTMENTS

Association of Investment Trust Companies (AITC)
Durrant House, 8–13 Chiswell Street, London EC1Y 4YY
0171 588 5347

Association of Policy Market Makers
Holywell Centre, 1 Phipp Street, London EC2A 4PS
0171 739 3949
(for a list of companies selling second-hand endowments)

Association of Solicitor Investment Managers (ASIM)
Baldocks, Chiddingstone Causeway, Tonbridge, Kent TN11 8JX
01892 870065

Association of Private Client Investment Managers
112 Middlesex Street, London E1 7HY.
0171 247 7080

Association of Unit Trusts and Investment Funds (AUTIF)
Information Unit, 65 Kingsway, London WC2B 6TD
0171 831 0898

National Savings Information
Room 073, Charles House, 376 Kensington High Street, London W14 8SD
0645 645000

ProShare
Library Chambers, 13–14 Basinghall Street, London EC2V 5BQ
0171 600 0984

Stock Exchange
Old Broad Street, London EC2N 1HP
0171 588 2355

BANKS AND BUILDING SOCIETIES

British Bankers' Association
105–108 Old Broad Street London EC2N 1EX
0171 216 8800

Banking Ombudsman
70 Grays Inn Road, London WC1X 8NB
0171 404 9944

Building Societies Association/Council of Mortgage Lenders
3 Savile Row, London W1X 1AF
0171 437 0655

Building Societies Ombudsman
Millbank Tower, Millbank, London SW1P 4XS
0171 931 0044

PENSIONS

Association of Consulting Actuaries (ACA)
1 Wardrobe Place, London EC4V 5AH
0171 248 3163

TAX

Occupational Pensions Advisory Service
11 Belgrave Road,
London SW1V 1RB
0171 233 8080

Pensions Ombudsman
11 Belgrave Road,
London SW1V 1RB
0171 834 9144

CREDIT REFERENCE AGENCIES

CCN Group Ltd
Consumer Help Service,
PO Box 40,
Nottingham NG7 2SS
0115 986 8172

Equifax Europe Ltd
Consumer Affairs Department,
Spectrum House, 1A North Avenue, Clydebank,
Glasgow G81 2DR
0141 951 1253

FINANCIAL ADVICE

Independent Financial Advice Promotion (IFAP)
4th Floor, 28 Greville Street,
London EC1N 8SU
0117 971 1177
(for a list of three independent advisers in your area)

Institute of Financial Planning
Whitefriars Centre,
Lewins Mead,
Bristol BS1 2NT
0117 930 4434

TAX AND ACCOUNTANCY

Adjudicator's Office,
3rd Floor,
Haymarket House,
28 Haymarket,
London SW1Y 4SP.
0171 930 2292

Capital Taxes Office
Ferrers House
PO Box 38,
Castle Meadow Road,
Nottingham NG2 1BB
0115 974 2424

Capital Taxes Office,
16 Picardy Place,
Edinburgh EH1 3NB
0131 556 8511

Capital Taxes Office,
Dorchester House,
52–58 Great Victoria Street,
Belfast BT2 7BB
01232 315556

Chartered Association of Certified Accountants (CACA)
29 Lincoln's Inn Fields,
London WC2A 3EE
0171 242 6855

Inland Revenue
Somerset House,
London WC2R 1LB
0171 438 6420
(or look in the phone book for your local tax office)

Institute of Chartered Accountants in England and Wales (ICAEW)
Chartered Accountants Hall,
PO Box 433, Moorgate Place,
London EC2P 2BJ
0171 920 8100

Institute of Chartered Accountants in Scotland (ICAS)
27 Queen Street,
Edinburgh EH2 1LA
0131 225 5673

TaxAid
342 Kilburn High Road,
London NW6 2QJ
0171 624 3768 (9am–11am)
(for free tax advice)

INSURANCE

Association of British Insurers (ABI)
51 Gresham Street,
London EC2V 7HQ
0171 600 3333

British Investment Insurance Brokers Association (BIIBA)
14 Bevis Marks,
London EC3A 7NT
0171 623 9043

Insurance Brokers Registration Council (IBRC)
63 St Mary Axe,
London EC3A 8NB
0171 621 1061

Insurance Ombudsman Bureau
City Gate One, 135 Park Street,
London SE1 9EA
0171 928 4488

LAW

Law Society
113 Chancery Lane,
London WC2A 1PL
0171 242 1222

Law Society of Scotland
26 Drumsheugh Gardens,
Edinburgh EH3 7YR
0131 226 7411

Legal Services Ombudsman
22 Oxford Court,
Oxford Street,
Manchester M2 3WQ
0161 236 9532

Office for the Supervision of Solicitors
Victoria Court, 8 Dormer Place,
Leamington Spa,
Warwickshire CV32 5AE
01926 820082

CONSUMER AFFAIRS

Citizens Advice Bureau (CAB)
Myddleton House,
115–123 Pentonville Road,
London N1 9LZ
0171 833 2181 (or Yellow Pages)

Consumers' Association
2 Marylebone Road,
London NW1 4DF
0171 830 6000

Help the Aged
St James's Walk,
London EC1R 0BE
0171 253 0253

Money Advice Association
1st Floor, Gresham House,
24 Holborn Viaduct,
London EC1A 2BN
0171 236 3566

National Debtline
318 Summer Lane,
Birmingham B19 3RL
0121 359 8501

National Gas Consumers Council
6th Floor, Abford House,
15 Wilton Road,
London SW1V 1LT
0171 931 0977

Office of Electricity Regulation (OFFER)
Hagley House,
Hagley Road,
Edgbaston B16 8QG
0121 456 2100

Office of Fair Trading (OFT)
Field House,
15–25 Bream's Buildings,
London EC4A 1PR
0345 224499

Office of Gas Supply (OFGAS)
130 Wilton Road,
London SW1V 1LQ
0171 828 0898

Office of Telecommunications Services (OFTEL)
Export House,
50 Ludgate Hill,
London EC4M 7JJ
0171 822 1650

Office of Water Services (OFWAT)
Centre City Tower,
7 Hill Street,
Birmingham B5 4UA
0121 625 1300

Trading Standards Coordinating Body
PO Box 6, Fell Road,
Croydon
CR9 1LG
0181 688 1996
(or look in the phone book for your local office)

BENEFITS

Age Concern
Astral House,
1268 London Road,
London SW16 4ER
0181 679 8000
(or look in the phone book for your local office)

Benefits Agency
For advice on most social security benefits look for your local office in the phone book under Benefits Agency or Social Security

Disability Benefits
The Benefit Enquiry Line is open for people with disabilities and their carers
0800 882200

National Association for Widows
54–57 Allison Street,
Digbeth,
Birmingham B5 5TH
0121 643 8348

Office of Social Security Commissioners
83–86 Farringdon Street,
London EC4A 1PR
0171 353 5145

CHARITY

Charities Aid Foundation (CAF)
Kings Hill,
West Malling,
Kent ME19 4TA.
01732 520000

Index

accountancy fees, allowability 157
accounting year 155
  definition 61–2
action plans
  capital gains tax 131
  complaints and enquiries 193
  home and family 49
  inheritance tax 141
  overpayment avoidance 15
  pensions 121
  record keeping 25
  savings and investments 93
  work 67
additional personal allowances 38
  tax returns 175
additional voluntary contributions
  (AVCs) 108–9, 171
Adjudicators 188–90
  leaflets 205
allocation of interest election 45–6
allowable expenses 63–4, 157
allowances 37–43, 99–100
  CGT 91, 127
  children 41–2
  income tax calculation 183, 184
  separation and divorce 40–1
  tax returns 174–5
  time limits 22
alternative investment market
  (AIM) 85–6
annuities 84–5
  tax returns 171
annuity deferral 119–21
antiques etc. 89–90, 141
appeals 187
approved profit-sharing
  schemes 153
asset redistributions, IHT 135–7
assets 64
  CGT 123–31
  tax returns 161, 166–7
AVCs see additional voluntary
  contributions

balance sheet summaries, tax
  returns 161
basic details, tax 21–5
'bed-and-breakfasting' 91
benefits 43–4
  tax returns 171
benefits in kind see perks
blind person's allowances 38, 39

tax returns 175
Budget (July 1997) 95, 98–9, 104–5,
  116
business series, leaflets 202–4

calculation, income tax 181–5
calendars
  employed persons 32–3
  self-employed persons 34–5
capital allowances 63–4
  tax returns 159, 165
capital gains tax (CGT) 23
  allowances 91, 127
  deposit-based savings 72–8
  employer share schemes 57
  examples 127, 129
  exemptions 123–4
  expenses 124
  flowchart 17
  homes 48–9, 130–1
  inflation effects 124–6
  investments 69–70, 78–91,
    128–30
  leaflets 199–200, 203
  losses 126, 167
  outline 123–31
  reliefs 126
capital gains/losses, tax returns
  166–7
carry forward/carry back 113–16,
  173
CGT see capital gains tax
charities
  donation methods 24–5
  leaflets 205
  tax returns 173
cheap loans, perks 56
checklist, potentially taxable
  perks 58
children 41–2
Codes of Practice, leaflets 205
commissioners 187, 191–2
company cars, perks 54–5
complaints 188–90
construction industry 161
contracting out, SERPS 65–6, 118
contributions see pension
  contributions
Controllers, Inland Revenue 188–9
convertible bonds 80
corporate bonds 79–80
credits, National Insurance 66

current accounts 72

declaration, tax returns 179
deposit-based savings 72–8
derivatives 88
directors, perks 53
divorce see separation and divorce
documents see records
domestic circumstances 37–49

earnings 149
  cap, pension schemes 103, 113
  limits 65–6
employers pensions 102–10
  AVCs 108–9, 171
  contributions 103–4
  growth 104–5
  income 105–6
  lump sums 106–7
  surpluses 105
  unapproved schemes 108
employment 51–60
  perks 53–8
  supplementary pages 146–53
  tax calendar 32–3
  working abroad 59–60
enquiries 190–2, 193
Enterprise Investment Scheme
  (EIS) 70, 71, 89
estate valuation, IHT 141
expenses
  allowability 63–4, 157
  CGT 124
  home working 48
  property letting 47–8
  tax returns 147, 149, 155–7, 165
  working abroad 60

final salary schemes 102, 105
fixed-interest investments 78–80
flowcharts
  overpayment 16
  savings/investments 18
  tax returns 19
  tax types 17
foreign earnings, tax returns 149
forms see P series; R85
Friendly Society savings plans or
  bonds 83
furnished holiday lettings, tax
  returns 163
futures 88

INDEX

general leaflets 200–3
gifts
  CGT 123–4, 126
  IHT 133–4, 136–7
gilts 78–9
government income, pie chart (1997-98) 21

help/guidance
  IHT 140
  income tax calculation 185
  tax returns 28, 144–5
higher personal allowances 42
holiday lettings, tax returns 163
homes 44–9, 167
  CGT 130–1
  IHT 136–7
  rental income 46–8
  workplaces 48–9

IHT *see* inheritance tax
income
  calculation 182–3
  growth bonds 83–4
  rents 46–8
  tax returns 147, 155–7, 165, 168–71
income tax 23, 91–2
  calculation 181–5
  deposit-based savings 72–8
  fixed-interest investments 78–80
  insurance-based investments 80–5
  investments 69–70
  leaflets 195–7
  offshore investments 92–3
  other investments 89–90
  pensions 99–100
  stockmarket investments 85–8
index-linked gilts 79
inflation effects, CGT 124–6
inheritance tax (IHT) 23
  asset redistributions 135–7
  calculation 134
  exemptions 133–4
  flowchart 17
  homes 136–7
  investments 69–70
  joint ownership 141
  leaflets 204
  life insurance 136, 140
  marriage 40, 135–6
  outline 133–41
  professional advice 140
  reduction 135–9
  trusts 136, 137–9

Inland Revenue
see also leaflets; self assessment;
  tax returns
  complaints 188–90
  enquiries 190–2, 193
  key areas 27–35
  meetings 191, 193
  mistakes 192–3
  notice of chargeability 143
  outline 21–2
  paperwork 28–30
insurance-based investments 80–5
interest charges 30–1, 192, 193
interest election, allocation of 45–6
international series, leaflets 204
investment trusts 86–7
investments
  CGT 128–30
  fixed-interest 78–80
  insurance-based 80–5
  leaflets 198–9
  marriage 39
  offshore 92–3
  outline 69–93
  pension funds 95, 98–9, 104–5, 116
  risk categories 71
  stockmarket 85–8
  tax returns 169
  tax-efficiency 14, 18, 90–2

land and property, supplementary pages 162–5
later years 42–3
leaflets
  Adjudicators 205
  CGT 199–200, 203
  charities 205
  Codes of Practice 205
  employee share schemes 198
  general business 202–3
  general tax matters 200–2
  IHT 204
  income tax 195–7
  international series 204
  savings and investments 198–9
  self assessment 202
  self-employment 203–4
liabilities, tax returns 161
life insurance 80–4, 91–2, 171
  IHT 136, 140
local authority bonds 80
losses
  CGT 126
  property letting 48
  setting off 64

tax returns 159, 165, 167
lump sums
  employers pensions 106–7
  personal pensions 116–17
  tax returns 149

maintenance payments 40–1
marriage 37–40, 90–1
  IHT 135–6
  MIRAS 45–6
married couple's allowances 22, 37–8, 42, 90–1
  tax returns 175
MIRAS *see* mortgage interest relief at source
money purchase schemes 102–3, 105
mortgages
  interest relief at source (MIRAS) 45–6, 130
  reliefs 44–6
  separation and divorce 40

National Insurance 65–6, 101–2
  tax returns 161
National Savings
  Capital Bonds 75
  Certificates 75
  Children's Bonus Bonds 75–6
  FIRST Option Bonds 76
  Income Bonds 76
  Index-Linked Certificates 76–7
  Investment Accounts 77
  Ordinary Accounts 77
  Pensioners Bonds (Granny Bonds) 77–8
  Premium Bonds 78
net relevant earnings 112–13
notice of calculation 29
notice of coding 28, 32–3, 100
  outline 51–3

offshore investments 92–3
options 88
overlap relief 61–2
overpayment
  avoidance 15
  flowchart 16
  tax flowchart 14
  tax returns 177

P11D forms 25, 32–3, 147
P45 forms 25, 53, 147
P46 forms 52–3
P60 forms 25, 32–3, 147, 171
pay as you earn (PAYE) 51–3

213

payments on account 29, 62, 192
penalties
　incomplete tax returns 179
　outline 30–1
　types 192
pension contributions 108–9, 171
　employers pensions 103–4
　personal pensions 111–16, 173
　tax relief 96–7
　tax returns 173
pensions 65–6
　annuities 84–5
　Budget (July 1997) 95, 98–9, 104–5, 116
　income tax 99–100
　life insurance 91–2
　outline 95–121
　tax returns 171
PEPs *see* personal equity plans
perks 52
　cheap loans 56
　company cars 54–5
　outline 53–8
　potential taxables checklist 58
　share schemes 56–7
　tax returns 147, 151, 153
permanent interest-bearing shares (PIBS) 79
personal allowances 37–9, 41–2, 99–100, 175
personal details, tax returns 177
personal equity plans (PEPs) 70, 71, 87–8
personal pensions 110–21
　annuity deferral 121
　contributions 111–13, 173
　extra contributions 113–16
　income 116
　lump sums 116–17
potentially exempt transfers 133
professional advice, IHT 140
property letting 46–8
　tax returns 162–5
purchased life annuities 107, 117

R85 forms 41
rates 23
　income tax calculation 183
record keeping
　enquiries 191, 193
　legal requirements 25, 30, 61
　penalties 31, 192
　tax returns 155
refunds, tax returns 177
reliefs 44–6, 91, 130
　CGT 126

charity donations 24–5
income tax calculation 182, 184
pension contributions 96–7, 103–4, 110–13
tax returns 149, 172–3
rent-a-room scheme 46–7
　tax returns 163
rental income 46–8
residency 43, 59–60
retail prices index (RPI), table 125
retirement annuities, tax returns 171
retirement annuity contracts 119

saving money 15, 90–2
savings
　deposit-based 72–8
　leaflets 198–9
　outline 69–93
　tax returns 169
　tax-efficiency 14, 18
segmented personal pensions 118
self assessment 13–14
　calendars 32–5
　income tax calculation 181–5
　leaflets 202
　outline 28–31
　transitional rules 62, 155
self-employment 60–5
　accounting year 61–2
　calendar 34–5
　leaflets 203–4
　supplementary pages 154–61
self-invested personal pensions (SIPPs) 118–19
separation and divorce 40–1
SERPS *see* state earnings-related pension scheme
share schemes
　leaflets 198
　perks 56–7
　supplementary pages 150–3
shares 79, 85–6
　see also investments
short-life assets 64
stamp duty 46
state earnings-related pension scheme (SERPS) 65–6, 118
state pensions 101–2
　tax returns 171
statements of account 29, 32–5
stockmarket investments 85–8
supplementary pages
　capital gains 166–7
　employment 146–53
　land and property 162–5

overview 143–5
self-employment 154–61
share schemes 150–3
Tax Calculation Guides 181–2
tax returns 15
　see also supplementary pages
　allowances 174–5
　completion guidelines 143–79
　enquiries 190–2
　flowchart 19
　help/guidance 28, 144–5
　income 168–71
　other information 176–9
　reliefs 149, 172–3
tax year, definition 22
Tax-Exempt Special Savings Accounts (TESSAs) 73–5
taxable profits, calculation 63–4
Taxpayers Charter 31
tenants in common 136–7
term accounts and bonds 73
TESSAs *see* Tax-Exempt Special Savings Accounts
time limits 22, 192
transitional allowances 175
transitional rules, self assessment 62, 155
trusts
　employers pensions 109–10
　IHT 136, 137–9

underpayment, tax returns 179
unit trusts 86

value added tax (VAT) 64–5
Venture Capital Trusts (VCTs) 71, 89

widow's bereavement allowances 38
　tax returns 175
work 51–67
　abroad 59–60
　homes 48–9

zero-dividend preference shares (zeros) 87

214